国家社会科学基金重大项目

“中国核心术语国际影响力研究”（21&ZD158）

“十四五”国家重点出版物出版规划项目

获评第二届向全国推荐中华优秀传统文化普及图书

Key Concepts in Chinese Thought and Culture

中华思想文化术语 10

《中华思想文化术语》编委会 编

外语教学与研究出版社
FOREIGN LANGUAGE TEACHING AND RESEARCH PRESS
北京 BEIJING

图书在版编目（CIP）数据

中华思想文化术语．10 ：汉英对照 ／《中华思想文化术语》编委会编．-- 北京 ：外语教学与研究出版社，2021.12

ISBN 978-7-5213-3239-1

Ⅰ．①中… Ⅱ．①中… Ⅲ．①中华文化－术语－汉、英 Ⅳ．①K203-61

中国版本图书馆 CIP 数据核字（2021）第 263203 号

出 版 人　王　芳
责任编辑　刘　佳
责任校对　刘虹艳
装帧设计　孙莉明
出版发行　外语教学与研究出版社
社　　址　北京市西三环北路 19 号（100089）
网　　址　http://www.fltrp.com
印　　刷　三河市北燕印装有限公司
开　　本　787×1092　1/16
印　　张　12
版　　次　2022 年 1 月第 1 版　2022 年 1 月第 1 次印刷
书　　号　ISBN 978-7-5213-3239-1
定　　价　48.00 元

购书咨询：（010）88819926　电子邮箱：club@fltrp.com
外研书店：https://waiyants.tmall.com
凡印刷、装订质量问题，请联系我社印制部
联系电话：（010）61207896　电子邮箱：zhijian@fltrp.com
凡侵权、盗版书籍线索，请联系我社法律事务部
举报电话：（010）88817519　电子邮箱：banquan@fltrp.com
物料号：332390001

记载人类文明
沟通世界文化
www.fltrp.com

“中华思想文化术语传播工程”专家团队

（按音序）

Scholars Participating in the Project “Key Concepts in Chinese Thought and Culture: Communication Through Translation”

顾问（Advisors）

李学勤（Li Xueqin）	林戊荪（Lin Wusun）
叶嘉莹（Florence Chia-ying Yeh）	张岂之（Zhang Qizhi）
楼宇烈（Lou Yulie）	王　宁（Wang Ning）

专家委员会（Committee of Scholars）

主任（Director）

韩　震（Han Zhen）

委员（Members）

晁福林（Chao Fulin）	陈德彰（Chen Dezhang）
陈明明（Chen Mingming）	冯志伟（Feng Zhiwei）
韩经太（Han Jingtai）	黄友义（Huang Youyi）
金元浦（Jin Yuanpu）	静　炜（Jing Wei）
李建中（Li Jianzhong）	李雪涛（Li Xuetao）
李照国（Li Zhaoguo）	聂长顺（Nie Changshun）
潘公凯（Pan Gongkai）	王　博（Wang Bo）

王柯平（Wang Keping）
叶　朗（Ye Lang）
袁济喜（Yuan Jixi）
袁行霈（Yuan Xingpei）
张　晶（Zhang Jing）
张立文（Zhang Liwen）
张西平（Zhang Xiping）
郑述谱（Zheng Shupu）

特邀汉学家（Scholars of China Studies）

艾　恺（Guy Salvatore Alitto）
安乐哲（Roger T. Ames）
白罗米（Luminița Bălan）
包华石（Martin Joseph Powers）
陈瑞河（Madaras Réka）
狄伯杰（B. R. Deepak）
顾　彬（Wolfgang Kubin）
韩安德（Harry Anders Hansson）
韩　裴（Petko Todorov Hinov）
柯鸿冈（Paul Crook）
柯马凯（Michael Crook）
斯巴修（Iljaz Spahiu）
王健、李盈（Jan & Yvonne Walls）
魏查理（Charles Willemen）

学术委员会（Academic Committee）

白振奎（Bai Zhenkui）
蔡力坚（Cai Lijian）
陈海燕（Chen Haiyan）
陈少明（Chen Shaoming）
程景牧（Cheng Jingmu）
丁　浩（Ding Hao）
付志斌（Fu Zhibin）
干春松（Gan Chunsong）
郭晓东（Guo Xiaodong）
韩志华（Han Zhihua）
何　淼（He Miao）
何世剑（He Shijian）
胡　海（Hu Hai）
贾德忠（Jia Dezhong）
姜海龙（Jiang Hailong）
黎　臻（Li Zhen）
李存山（Li Cunshan）
李恭忠（Li Gongzhong）

李景林（Li Jinglin）
林少阳（Lin Shaoyang）
刘　璐（Liu Lu）
吕玉华（Lü Yuhua）
孟庆楠（Meng Qingnan）
彭冬林（Peng Donglin）
任大援（Ren Dayuan）
沈卫星（Shen Weixing）
陶黎庆（Tao Liqing）
王丽丽（Wang Lili）
王明杰（Wang Mingjie）
王　鑫（Wang Xin）
吴根友（Wu Genyou）
夏　晶（Xia Jing）
辛红娟（Xin Hongjuan）
徐亚男（Xu Yanan）
严学军（Yan Xuejun）
张子尧（Zhang Ziyao）
章伟文（Zhang Weiwen）
赵　悠（Zhao You）
周云帆（Zhou Yunfan）
朱良志（Zhu Liangzhi）
左　励（Zuo Li）
林敏洁（Lin Minjie）
刘　佳（Liu Jia）
刘　青（Liu Qing）
梅缵月（Mei Zuanyue）
裴德思（Thorsten Pattberg）
乔　希（Joshua Mason）
邵亦鹏（Shao Yipeng）
施晓菁（Lynette Shi）
童孝华（Tong Xiaohua）
王　琳（Wang Lin）
王维东（Wang Weidong）
温海明（Wen Haiming）
吴礼敬（Wu Lijing）
谢远笋（Xie Yuansun）
徐明强（Xu Mingqiang）
许家星（Xu Jiaxing）
张　静（Zhang Jing）
章思英（Zhang Siying）
赵　桐（Zhao Tong）
郑　开（Zheng Kai）
朱绩崧（Zhu Jisong）
朱　渊（Zhu Yuan）

前言

“中华思想文化术语”的定义可以表述为：由中华民族所创造或构建，凝聚、浓缩了中华哲学思想、人文精神、思维方式、价值观念，以词或短语形式固化的概念和文化核心词。它们是中华民族几千年来对自然与社会进行探索和理性思索的成果，积淀着中华民族的历史智慧，反映中华民族最深沉的精神追求以及理性思索的深度与广度；其所蕴含的人文思想、思维方式、价值观念已经作为一种“生命基因”深深融于中华子孙的血液，内化为中华民族共同的性格和信仰，并由此支撑起中华数千年的学术传统、思想文化和精神世界。它是当代中国人理解中国古代哲学思想、人文精神、思维方式、价值观念之变化乃至文学艺术、历史等各领域发展的核心关键，也是世界其他国家和民族了解当代中国、中华民族和海外华人之精神世界的钥匙。

当今世界已进入文化多元与话语多极时代。世界不同区域、不同国家、不同民族的文明，其流动融合之快、之广、之深超过历史任何时期。每个国家和民族都有自己独具的思想文化和话语体系，都应在世界文明、世界话语体系中占有一席之地，得到它应有的地位和尊重。而思想文化术语无疑是一个国家和民族话语体系中最核心、最本质的部分，是它的思想之“髓”、文化之“根”、精神之“魂”、学术之“核”。越来越多的有识之士认识到，中华思想文化蕴藏着解决当今人类所面临的许多难题的重要启示，中华民族所倡导的“厚德载物”“道法自然”“天人合一”“和而不同”“民惟邦本”“经世致用”等思想，以及它所追求的“协和万邦”“天下一家”、世界“大同”，代表了当今世界文明的发展趋势，也因此成为国际社会的共识。越来越多的外国学者和友人对中华思想文化及其术语产生浓厚的兴趣，希望有更全面、更进一步的了解。

今天我们整理、诠释、翻译、传播中华思想文化术语，目的是立足于中华思想文化，通过全面系统的整理与诠释，深度挖掘其中既能反映中华哲学思想、人文精神、思维方式、价值观念、文化特征，又具跨越时空、超越国度之意义，以及富有永恒魅力与当代价值的含义和内容，并将其译成英语等语言，让世界更客观、更全面地认识中国，了解中华民族的过去和现在，了解当代中国人及海外华人的精神世界，从而推动国家间的平等对话及不同文明间的交流借鉴。

中华思想文化术语的整理、诠释和英语翻译得到了中国教育部、中国国际出版集团、中央编译局、北京大学、中国人民大学、武汉大学、北京外国语大学等单位的大力支持，得到了叶嘉莹、李学勤、张岂之、林戊荪、楼宇烈、王宁等海内外众多知名学者的支持。需要说明的是，“中华思想文化术语”这个概念是首次提出，其内涵和外延还有待学界更深入的研究；而且，如此大规模地整理、诠释、翻译中华思想文化术语，在中国也是首次，无成例可循。因此，我们的诠释与翻译一定还有待完善的地方，我们会及时吸纳广大读者的意见，不断提高术语诠释与翻译的质量。

2021 年 12 月 11 日

Foreword

By "key concepts in Chinese thought and culture" we mean concepts and keywords or phrases the Chinese people have created or come to use and that are fundamentally pertinent to Chinese philosophy, humanistic spirit, way of thinking, and values. They represent the Chinese people's exploration of and rational thinking about nature and society over thousands of years. These concepts and expressions reflect the Chinese people's wisdom, their profound spiritual pursuit, as well as the depth and width of their thinking. Their way of thinking, values, and philosophy embodied in these concepts have become a kind of "life gene" in Chinese culture, and have long crystallized into the common personality and beliefs of the Chinese nation. For the Chinese people today, they serve as a key to a better understanding of the evolutions of their ancient philosophy, humanistic spirit, way of thinking, and values as well as the development of Chinese literature, art, and history. For people in other countries, these concepts open the door to understanding the spiritual world of contemporary China and the Chinese people, including those living overseas.

In the era of cultural diversity and multipolar discourse today, cultures of different countries and civilizations of different peoples are integrating faster, in greater depth, and on a greater scope than ever before. All countries and peoples have their own systems of thought, culture, and discourse, which should all have their place in the civilization and discourse systems of the world. They all deserve due respect. The concepts in thought and culture of a country and its people are naturally the most essential part of their discourse. They constitute the marrow of a nation's thought, the root of its culture, the soul of its spirit, and the core of its scholarship. More and more people of vision have come to recognize the inspirations Chinese thought and culture might offer to help resolve many difficult problems faced by mankind. The Chinese hold that a man should "have ample virtue and carry all things," "Dao operates naturally," "heaven and man are united as one," a man of virtue seeks "harmony but not uniformity," "people are the foundation of the state," and "study of ancient classics should meet present needs." The Chinese ideals such as "coexistence of all in harmony," "all the people under heaven are one family," and a world of "universal harmony" are drawing increasing attention among the international community. More and more international scholars and friends have become interested in learning and better understanding Chinese thought and culture in general, and the relevant concepts in particular.

In selecting, explaining, translating, and sharing concepts in Chinese thought and culture, we have adopted a comprehensive and systematic approach. Most of them not only reflect the characteristics of Chinese philosophy, humanistic spirit, way of thinking, values, and culture, but also have significance and/or implications that transcend time and national boundaries, and that still fascinate present-day readers and offer them food for thought. It is hoped that the translation of these concepts into English and other languages will help people in other countries to gain a more objective and more rounded understanding of China, of its people, of its past and present, and of the spiritual world of contemporary Chinese. Such understanding should be conducive to promoting equal dialogue between China and other countries and exchanges between different civilizations.

The selection, explanation, and translation of these concepts have been made possible thanks to the support of the Ministry of Education, China International Publishing Group, the Central Compilation and Translation Bureau, Peking University, Renmin University of China, Wuhan University, and Beijing Foreign Studies University, as well as the support of renowned scholars in China and abroad, including Florence Chia-ying Yeh, Li Xueqin, Zhang Qizhi, Lin Wusun, Lou Yulie, and Wang Ning.

The idea of compiling key concepts in Chinese thought and culture represents an innovation and the project calls much research and effort both in connotation and denotation. Furthermore, an endeavor like this has not been previously attempted on such a large scale. Lack of precedents means there must remain much room for improvement. Therefore, we welcome comments from all readers in the hope of better fulfilling this task.

December 11, 2021

目录
Contents

āilè-zhōngjié 哀乐中节

Express Grief and Joy in Accordance with the Rules of Propriety

喜怒哀乐的表达都符合法度。既能充分地表达情绪情感，又不偏激乖戾，由情而发，而以礼约束。这一术语可用作人生哲学，也可用于艺术创作，其核心思想为儒家的中庸原则，不偏不倚，无过无不及，一切都恰到好处。由此而从事作文、写诗、绘画等文艺创作活动，其作品自然会呈现均衡的中和之美，也符合温柔敦厚的教化之义。

This term holds that all expressions of grief and joy should be kept under the restraint of propriety. It means that artists should not be extreme when giving vent to their feelings. They should start off with feelings but end in self-discipline. The term applies to both the philosophical field and artistic creation. What it accentuates is the golden mean, a Confucian term advocating impartiality, reconciliation, and compromise, with propriety as its overriding principle. If an artist obeys the golden mean, whether he writes an essay or a poem or paints a picture, his work will naturally show the beauty of equilibrium and highlight the gentleness and honesty of the Confucian doctrine.

引例 Citations：

◎喜怒哀乐之未发，谓之中；发而皆中（zhòng）节，谓之和。中也者，天下之大本也；和也者，天下之达道也。致中和，天地位焉，万物育焉。（《礼记·中庸》）

（喜怒哀乐还没有被事物感发时的状态，称作“中”；喜怒哀乐表现于言行而都能符合规范，称作“和”。“中”是天下的根本，“和”是天下最普遍的法则。治理者能够达到“中和”，天地就能处于正位，万物便可生长繁育了。）

When joy, anger, sorrow, or happiness is not yet expressed in response to an event, it is known as a state of balance. When they are expressed in words and deeds within the scope of propriety, harmony is achieved. Balance is the foundation of all things under heaven, while harmony is the universal rule. If a ruler can achieve balanced harmony, both heaven and earth will be in their proper places, and all things will prosper and thrive. (*The Book of Rites*)

◎喜怒哀乐，情也。其未发，则性也，无所偏倚，故谓之中。发皆中节，情之正也，无所乖戾，故谓之和。（朱熹《中庸章句》）

（喜怒哀乐，是人类的情感。当它们没有表达出来的时候，属于自然天性，没有特殊的偏向，所以称作“中”。当它们表达出来而都能符合规范，情感中正，没有乖违偏激的情况，所以称作“和”。）

Happiness, anger, sorrow, and joy are the common manifestations of human feelings. When kept undisclosed, they constitute a natural instinct and are regarded as “impartial.” When they are displayed, and in accordance with the rules of propriety, without any trace of extremity, they are regarded as “harmonious.” (Zhu Xi: *Annotations on The Doctrine of the Mean*)

ānmín 安民

Give Peace and Comfort to the People

安定百姓或让百姓安居乐业。中国古人认为，这是国家或治国理政者的基本职责和主要目标，也是执政者赢得民众拥护的基本前提，同时也是降低治理成本、争取更好治理状态的基础条件。而“安民”的根本在于保障百姓的实际利益，及时地发现、匡正政策或制度的缺失。这与“民惟邦本”的思想是息息相通的。

The term means to ensure that the people live and work in peace and contentment. The ancients believed that this was the basic responsibility and main purpose of the state and of those governing it. A peaceful and satisfied populace results in widespread support for the rulers, making governance less costly and more effective. The heart of the concept is to guarantee the genuine interests of the people, and to identify and correct failings in both policies and procedures in a timely way. The expression mirrors the concept "people are the foundation of the state."

引例 Citations:

◎安民则惠，黎民怀之。(《尚书·皋陶（yáo）谟》)

（安定百姓，给他们恩惠，这样百姓就会拥戴他。）

His kindness satisfied the people, so they supported him. (*The Book of History*)

◎为治之本，务在于安民；安民之本，在于足用。(《淮南子·诠言训》)

（治国理政的根本，在于努力安定百姓；安定百姓的根本，在于努力使财用富足。）

State governance is based on a populace living in peace and contentment, which in turn is based on material sufficiency. (*Huainanzi*)

◎安民可与行义，而危民易与为非。(《史记·秦始皇本纪》)

（安居乐业的百姓可以与他们一起践行仁义，而身处危境的百姓则容易为非作歹。）

A contented populace can be benevolent and righteous, but one under threat can be immoral and evil. (*Records of the Historian*)

bēimǐn 悲悯

Mercy and Compassion

慈悲怜悯。即哀人之哀，痛人之痛。它是佛教“慈悲”与儒家“恻隐”思想的融合。“悲”即“慈悲”，佛教认为，给予众生安乐为“慈”，拔除众生痛苦为“悲”；“悯”即怜悯，与“恻隐”义近，意思是对他人的不幸由衷同情，不忍漠视。合在一起，指对他人或世人的痛苦或灾难感同身受，力图把他人从痛苦或灾难中救拔出来，使之安宁快乐。这种真诚的仁爱、博大的胸怀，源于人的天赋情感的道德境界，是杰出人物挺身担当的精神原动力。

This term means to feel sad for others' sadness and feel painful for others' suffering. It is a combination of the Buddhist concept of "mercy" and Confucian concept of "compassion." "Mercy" in Buddhism implies both kind-heartedness that brings peace and happiness to all and sympathy that relieves others from their misery. "Compassion" means sympathizing with people from the bottom of one's heart over their misfortunes. Put together, they describe a noble mindset that takes other people's suffering as one's own, commiserates with the unfortunate while trying one's best to free people from their miseries or disasters, and helps them to regain their peace and happiness. This kind of true benevolence and noble mind comes from a human being's innate moral sense and is the source of the spiritual force that drives noble and eminent personalities.

引例 Citations：

◎无恻隐之心，非人也。……恻隐之心，仁之端也。（《孟子·公孙丑上》）

（没有恻隐之心，就不能算人。……恻隐之心是仁的端始。）

Those who do not have compassion are not human beings... Having compassion is the incipient stage of benevolence. (*Mencius*)

◎现自在端严相，起利他悲悯心。（释法薰《赞水月观音》）

（现出安闲端庄的法相，开启［世人］施惠他人的悲悯情怀。）

(Guanyin, the Goddess of Mercy, is portrayed as) calm and dignified in appearance, capable of inspiring benevolence and compassion in a viewer's heart. (Shi Faxun: Exalting the Picture of Guanyin with a Backdrop of Water and the Moon)

◎圣人以悲悯为心，不取沮溺之忘世。（王永彬《围炉夜话》）

（圣人有慈悲怜悯的胸怀，不像长沮、桀溺两位隐士那样避世不顾。）

Unlike the hermits Chang Ju and Jie Ni who shunned the world, sages cherished mercy and compassion. (Wang Yongbin: *Night Talks Round the Hearth*)

bǐxiǎn-xìngyǐn 比显兴隐

Make Analogy Explicit and Association Implicit

“比”显豁而“兴”隐约。“比”与“兴”都源于《诗经》的六义。“比”是用一种事物比拟另一种事物，其目的是为了更好地传达思想情感，让人更透彻地知晓意思。因此，两种事物之间的相似特征应明确清晰、意义显豁，这样才容易被理解，否则就失去了“比”的意义。“兴”虽然同样由此及彼，但二者之间的关系是朦胧隐微的，由情感、韵味、氛围等形成内在的关联，没有明确的逻辑理路可寻。“比显兴隐”适用于诗歌创作，其中，“比”是切近的、明显的，使意义明白晓畅；“兴”则是深远的、隐蔽的，使审美韵味悠长。

Analogies in a literary work should be conveyed clearly, and associations, subtly. Examples of analogy and association were first found in the six basic elements of *The Book of Songs*. "Analogy" means comparing one thing to another in order to better express one's feelings and thoughts, thus making oneself more thoroughly understood. With this in view, similarities between two things should be made apparent and exact; otherwise, carrying out a comparison would become meaningless. "Association," too, compares one thing to another, but such a link is indirect and nuanced, created by an inner combination of sentiment, charm and atmosphere, without a traceable cause or logic. The notion of explicit analogy versus implicit association is widely applied to poetry creation. Specifically, analogy is adjacent, obvious and easily intelligible, whereas association is profound, covert and aesthetically pleasing.

引例 Citations：

◎《诗》文弘奥，包韫六义，毛公述传，独标"兴"体，岂不以"风"通而"赋"同，"比"显而"兴"隐哉！（刘勰《文心雕龙·比兴》）

（《诗经》中的作品宏大深奥，包含风、雅、颂、赋、比、兴六义。毛亨、毛苌为《诗经》作传，唯独标注了"兴"。难道不是因为"风"意义晓畅而"赋"铺陈直接、"比"显豁而"兴"隐约吗？）

Poetic works in *The Book of Songs* have both width and depth. They are represented by six basic elements: ballad, court hymn, eulogy, narrative, analogy and association. Mao Heng and Mao Chang, in interpreting *The Book of Songs*, singled out association for extra explanation. Isn't that because ballads are simple and crude, narratives are direct, analogies are obvious but associations obscure? (Liu Xie: *The Literary Mind and the Carving of Dragons*)

◎叙物以言情谓之赋，情物尽也；索物以托情谓之比，情附物者也；触物以

起情谓之兴，物动情者也。（胡寅《致李叔易》引李仲蒙语）

（描述事物以表达情感称为“赋”，“赋”对情感和物象的描写都很充分；寻求借助事物以寄托情感称为“比”，“比”的特点是情感须要依附某种物象；遇到某物偶然产生某种情感称为“兴”，“兴”的特点是物象激发情感。）

Narratives express inner feelings through describing external things; they give full expression to both feelings and objects. Analogies embody feelings in objects and attach feelings to objects. Associations are created through external things one sees by chance; in an association, feelings are inspired by objects. (As quoted in Hu Yin: A Letter to Li Shuyi)

bùchéng-wúwù 不诚无物

Without Sincerity, Nothing Is Possible.

没有诚，任何事物都不会存在。诚即真实、真诚。儒家认为，它是人和万事万物所遵循的基本原理或法则，是人和万事万物充分发挥其固有天性或本质属性的过程，是人和万事万物得以存在或完成其自身的终极依据，是人和万事万物达成的同步互动、有机融合的理想境界。单就人世层面来说，犹言若无诚心，则一事无成。这一命题表达了“诚”的实在性、终极性、人的主体性以及主客体的统一性。

Confucian scholars believed that nothing is possible without sincerity, which is the basic principle or law followed by humans and all things. It is a process in which humans and all things give full play to their inherent nature or essential properties. Sincerity is what enables them to exist and improve themselves, and it is an ideal state of both their interaction and integration. In terms of human activities, it is obvious that without sincerity, nothing can be accomplished. This notion stresses that sincerity is both real and fundamental, that humans have subjectivity, and that with sincerity, they can achieve unity with the outer world.

引例 Citations:

◎诚者自成也，而道自道（dǎo）也。诚者，物之终始。不诚无物。是故君子诚之为贵。诚者，非自成己而已也，所以成物也。成己，仁也；成物，知（zhì）也。性之德也，合外内之道也。（《礼记·中庸》）

（诚是自我完成，道是自我引导。诚贯穿事物发展的始终。没有诚，则任何事物都不会存在。所以君子特别崇尚诚。诚不只是自我完成，还要成就万事万物。完成自我是仁，成就万事万物是智。仁与智乃出于天性，是融合自身与外物的基本法则。）

Sincerity is what makes oneself whole, and its way shows how one conducts oneself. Sincerity makes things happen and deliver outcomes. Without sincerity, there is nothing. For this reason, a man of virtue reveres sincerity. Sincerity not only makes oneself whole but also makes other people and creatures whole. Making oneself whole is a virtue; making others whole is vision. Virtue and vision are naturally born, and they are fundamental to achieving unity between oneself and the outer world. (*The Book of Rites*)

◎诚者，物之终始。不诚无物。物者，事也。言不诚即无所事矣。（《新唐书·陆贽传》）

（诚贯穿事物发展的始终。没有诚，则任何事物都不会存在。物与事是一个意思。这句话是说，不诚就会一事无成。）

Sincerity makes things happen and delivers outcomes. Without sincerity, there is nothing. Things are the same as undertakings. Without sincerity, nothing can be achieved. (*The New Tang History*)

bùzhēng 不争

Not Engaging in Contention

不争夺，不争斗。个人对外物过度的欲求，会导致彼此之间的争夺。而无序的纷争则会造成道德的沦丧和社会秩序的混乱。因此，儒家和道家都主张“不争”。儒家主张一方面按照礼的规则，有差等地安顿并节制人的欲望；另一方面则通过道德教化，引导人们自省其过而不责备于人，由此实现“不争”。道家则主张通过君主的无为，以辅助百姓处于“不争”的状态。在道家思想中，“不争”有时特指道对待万物、为政者对待百姓的一种态度：道不与万物争，君主不与百姓争。

This refers to not contending for personal interest, power and other things and not involving in various infighting or strife. Excessive desire for material gains and power leads to contention, strife or even violence. Uncontrolled contention results in decline of public moral and breakdown of social order. This is why both Confucianism and Daoism believe in no contention. Confucianism maintains that rules of rites should be observed to restrain people's desire. People should be guided by moral education, and they should think about how to behave properly rather than shifting blame on others. Thus, a state of no contention can be reached. Daoism maintains that one in power should not interfere in the lives of people so as to encourage them not to engage in contention. According to Daoism, the term not engaging in contention sometimes refers to the attitude of Dao towards everything in the world and that of one in power towards the common people. Dao does not favor contention with anything, so a king should not contend with the people.

引例 Citations：

◎子云："善则称人，过则称己，则民不争。"（《礼记・坊记》）

（孔子说："做得好则称道他人，有过错则省察自己，则民众不争斗。"）

Confucius said: "If we think about others when we are successful and criticize our own shortcomings, people will not contend with each other." (*The Book of Rites*)

◎夫唯不争，故天下莫能与之争。（《老子・二十二章》）

（正因为不争，所以天下没有能够与之相抗争的。）

If one does not engage in contention, no others in the world can contend with him. (*Laozi*)

chéngxīn 成心

Biased Mind

带有成见的心。出自《庄子・齐物论》。庄子（前369?—前286）认为，人们如果站在自我立场上去看待他者，就会用自己的标准形成对他者、对世界的成见。而由于立场或标准的不同，彼此的成见会造成各种对立和纷争。被成见所遮蔽的心，就是"成心"。人们怀有"成心"而往往不自知。因此，庄子提示人们应意识到并超越"成心"以及狭隘的自我立场。

This refers to prejudice a person has developed towards a particular person or thing. The concept is from *Zhuangzi*. The author Zhuangzi (369?-286 BC) believed that people will develop biased views about other people or things when they only look at other people or things from their own perspectives. Such bias caused by different points of view or standards can lead to disagreement or confrontation. People seldom realize that they have a biased mind. Thus Zhuangzi suggested that people need to be aware of their own biased mind and overcome it.

引例 Citation:

◎夫随其成心而师之，谁独且无师乎？奚必知代而心自取者有之？愚者与有焉。未成乎心而有是非，是今日适越而昔至也。（《庄子·齐物论》）

（如果顺着自己带有成见的心而遵从它，那么谁还没有一个遵从的标准呢？为何一定是知道万物变化而心有见识的人才有呢？愚笨的人也是有的啊。没有在心中形成见识就已经有是非，这就好像今天到越国去但昨天已经到达了。）

If people just follow their own biased mind, does it mean that there are no general standards for all to follow? Both those well-informed people who know that everything changes and foolish people have biased minds. Claiming to know about what is right and wrong about something before gaining enough knowledge about it is like journeying to the State of Yue today and arriving there yesterday. (*Zhuangzi*)

chōngshí zhī wèi měi 充实之谓美

Moral Fulfillment Is Beauty Itself.

各种美好品德充实于内心就是美。出自《孟子·尽心下》。孟子（前

372？一前 289）对于美的本质的认识，与儒家的伦理道德密切相关。在孟子的美学思想中，“美”是人格评价序列“善、信、美、大、圣、神”当中的一级。“充实”喻示了道德圆满、和谐、完备的境界，当一个人被“善”“信”等品德充实，他必然具有强大的精神力量，而体现为人格之美。也可以说，美是一个人由道德伦理的自足升华为审美愉悦时的一种精神状态，代表了道德与审美一体的儒家人格理想，体现了美与善的高度统一。体现在文学批评中，它主要强调作家应培养浩然正气与美好品德，这样才能创造出具有崇高内在精神的作品。这一术语将内心道德的充实与否作为衡量作品高下的重要标准，目的在于倡导道德人格与艺术审美的和谐统一。

Moral fulfillment of one's mind and heart means beauty in character. This term comes from the book *Mencius*. Mencius' (372?-289 BC) understanding of beauty relates closely to Confucian morality. To his mind, beauty is one of the qualities on the rating scale for personality, which ranges from those of virtue, honorableness, beauty, magnanimity, saintliness, all the way up to the divine. Central to all these is moral fulfillment, which refers to the perfection, harmony and completeness of a person's moral well-being. When a person is enriched by virtue and honorableness, he is filled with tremendous moral strength and thus attains a beauty of personality. In other words, beauty is a spiritual state of worthiness achievable when moral self-sufficiency becomes elevated into an aesthetic ecstasy, reflecting the Confucian ideal of perfect harmony between morality and aesthetics, or that between beauty and goodness. In literary criticism, this is shown via the argument that a writer should strive to be upright before he can create noble-spirited works. This term sets moral fulfillment as an important criterion for judging the quality of a literary work, and advocates a unity between artistic excellence and moral well-being.

引例 Citations：

◎可欲之谓善，有诸己之谓信，充实之谓美，充实而有光辉之谓大，大而化之之谓圣，圣而不可知之之谓神。(《孟子·尽心下》)

（值得人们喜爱就是善，自己具备了善行就是信，各种美好品德充实于内心就是美，充实之后又能发扬光大称为大，既大而又能感化万物称为圣，圣明到了不可测度的神妙境地称为神。）

A person that is lovable can be called virtuous. He who is virtuous can be described as honorable. If his soul possesses moral goodness, it also possesses beauty. If that beauty can be made to spread afar, it becomes magnanimous. If that magnanimity can spread its influence across the whole world, he attains sainthood. If such sainthood can reach immeasurable heights, then he possesses the quality of the divine. (*Mencius*)

◎气以实志，志以定言；吐纳英华，莫非情性。（刘勰《文心雕龙·体性》）

（天生的气质禀赋使人具有充实的情志，情志决定文章的语言；文采的吸纳与文章是否精美，全都取决于人的真情实感。）

Natural inclination and character give an author an immense aspiration. This, in turn, determines the language of his writing. Literary grace and glory result solely from the author's true feelings. (Liu Xie: *The Literary Mind and the Carving of Dragons*)

chóngdé 崇德

Moral Elevation

提升品德。早期儒家的《论语》《周易》等文献中都提到“崇德”的观念。

儒家高度重视人的道德，而人的道德需要不断地提升和完善，这即是“崇德”的过程。人们可以通过对忠信等道德原则的坚守来修正自己的言行，以提升自身的道德修养。同时，只有在处事中不断磨炼，才能真正实现“崇德”。

This term refers to elevation of moral character, a concept which is first mentioned in early Confucian classics such as *The Analects* and *The Book of Changes*. Confucianism placed great emphasis on human morals, believing that such morals should be constantly fostered and elevated; and this is the process of moral elevation. By steadfastly observing the moral principles of loyalty and good faith, people can improve their pronouncements and deeds, thereby elevating their moral cultivation. Moral elevation can only be achieved through sustained efforts.

引例 Citations：

◎子曰：“主忠信，徙义，崇德也。”（《论语·颜渊》）
（孔子说：“以忠信为本，改易自己的言行以合于道义，就是提高德行。）

Confucius said, “To be loyal, act in good faith and change your pronouncements and deeds so as to do what is right – that is elevating moral character.” (*The Analects*)

◎夫《易》，圣人所以崇德而广业也。（《周易·系辞上》）
（圣人通过《周易》来提高德行、光大事业。）

The sage elevates people’s moral character and improves their deeds through *The Book of Changes*. (*The Book of Changes*)

dàqīngmíng 大清明

Great Clarity and Brightness

完全清晰透彻的认知状态。由荀子（前313？—前238）提出。荀子认为，人通过“心”的作用来认知人伦日用之道。但受到各种因素的影响，人心常处于被遮蔽的状态。荀子主张通过“虚壹而静”的方式，来解除“心”的遮蔽，实现对人伦日用之道清晰、透彻的认识。这一认知状态即是“大清明”。

This expression refers to a cognitive state which is completely clear and penetrating. It was proposed by Xunzi (313?-238 BC). He felt that people could understand human relations in daily life through the use of the “mind” (*xin* 心), but the mind was often clouded by various factors. Xunzi advocated lifting the clouds by keeping the mind open, concentrated and tranquil, which would lead to a clear and penetrating understanding of human relations in daily life. Such a cognitive state is that of great clarity and brightness.

引例 Citation:

◎虚壹而静，谓之大清明。（《荀子·解蔽》）

（心以虚壹而静的方式认知道，就称为“大清明”。）

Keeping the mind open, concentrated and tranquil when one tries to understand general rules – this is called great clarity and brightness. (*Xunzi*)

dàyǎn 大衍

The Fundamental Calculation

至极的演算。“大”指至极，“衍”指演算。“大衍”一词出自《周易·系辞上》。《系辞》说明了用五十根蓍草演算成卦的过程。占筮者要按照一定的规则反复分合蓍草，通过蓍草数量的变化来逐一确定各爻的阴阳，最终得出卦象。这种演算被认为模拟了天地万物生成变化的过程，并用以探求、把握事物发展的规则与趋势。

This refers to the fundamental oracular calculation. The term “fundamental calculation,” which is from *The Book of Changes*, refers to the procedure for creating hexagrams by using fifty yarrow stalks. The diviner would repeatedly combine and separate groups of yarrow stalks according to a set of rules. The changes in the numbers of the stalks were used to ascertain the yin and yang, namely, the negative and positive, characteristics of each trigram, and the trigrams were in turn used to form a hexagram. This method of calculation was believed to represent the process through which everything was created and evolved, and it was used to explore and understand the rules which govern changes and their underlying trends.

引例 Citation：

◎大衍之数五十，其用四十有九。（《周易·系辞上》）

（用来做至极演算的数是五十，使用的有四十九根蓍草。）

The number (of yarrow stalks) in the fundamental calculation is fifty, of which forty-nine are used. (*The Book of Changes*)

dàobùyùzá 道不欲杂

The Fundamental Principle Should Not Be a Mixture of Ideas.

道不宜混杂。道在这里指根本的、普遍的原则。也就是说，道应当是纯一的、一以贯之的。这是《庄子》所载孔子（前551—前479）的观点。庄子（前369？—前286）借孔子之口说：根本的、普遍的原则如果混杂而成，就会造成多种思想的分歧、干扰、冲突与混乱，将会引发难以挽回的灾难。运用于治理国家，它实际强调的是指导思想的纯洁性与一贯性。这与“大道至简”的思想不无相通之处。

This concept means that the fundamental principle known as Dao (the Way) should be pure and consistent. This was allegedly the view of Confucius (551–479 BC), as stated in the classic *Zhuangzi*. In the name of Confucius, Zhuangzi (369?-286BC) states that if the fundamental principle admits a mixture of ideas, there will be divergence, interference, conflict and confusion among them, and this will lead to great chaos. As it applies to governance of the state, this concept emphasizes the importance of purity and consistency of the guiding thought. It is similar to the concept that great truth is expressed in simple words.

引例 Citation:

◎夫道不欲杂，杂则多，多则扰，扰则忧，忧而不救。（《庄子·人间世》）

（道不宜混杂，混杂了，就等于有多重原则，它会造成思想纷扰，从而招致忧患，忧患多了也就难以救治。）

Dao (the Way) should not be allowed to become a mixture of all ideas. This will create confusion, which, in turn, will lead to chaos that is beyond control. (*Zhuangzi*)

dàoqì 道器

Dao and Objects

普遍的规律、原理和有形、具体的事物。这是中国古代哲学的一对重要范畴。“道”是“形而上”的，无形质的、隐没的；“器”是“形而下”的，有形质的，显现的。前者体现事物的普遍统一性，后者体现事物的特殊多样性。但二者并不是截然分开的，而是有着内在的一致性——前者是对后者的抽象，后者是前者的具体展现，两者是辩证统一的关系。

This concept means generally applicable principles and tangible concrete objects, which are an important pair of concepts in ancient Chinese philosophy. Dao is invisible, concealed and metaphysical, while objects are tangible, visible and physical. The former represents unity of things, while the latter demonstrates diversity of things. However, the two are not diametrically opposed to each other. Rather, they are inherently in unity in that the former is the abstraction of the latter, while the latter is the concrete manifestation of the former, and the two have a relationship of dialectical unity.

引例 Citations：

◎形而上者谓之道，形而下者谓之器。(《周易·系辞上》)
（未成形质者称为“道”，已成形质者称为“器”。）

What is above form is called Dao, and what is under form is called “an object.” (*The Book of Changes*)

◎道器无二，性在气质。（黄宗羲《明儒学案·江右王门学案一·文庄邹东廓先生守益》）

（道和器不是两不相干的东西，就像人的本性存在于气质之中一样。）

Dao and objects are interconnected, just as one's inherent qualities find expression in his temperament. (Huang Zongxi: *Commentaries on Writings of Famous Scholars of the Ming Dynasty*)

◎大抵会得时，道器隐显，有无本末一致。（黄宗羲《明儒学案·江右王门学案二·文庄欧阳南野先生德》）

（大体上贯通了，就明白“道”是隐没的、“器”是显现的，像“有”与“无”、“本”与“末”一样，二者本质上是一致的。）

Once someone gains a general understanding of things, he will realize that Dao is invisible and objects are visible, just as *you* (with form) as well as *wu* (without form) and *ben* (the fundamental) and *mo* (the incidental) each exists in relation to the other. (Huang Zongxi: *Commentaries on Writings of Famous Scholars of the Ming Dynasty*)

dàoshū 道枢

Pivot of Dao

道的关键。枢：关键，枢要。出自《庄子·齐物论》。庄子（前369？—前286）指出，人们往往会站在自我立场、以自己的标准去看待他者。而由于立场或标准的不同，人们对彼此、对事物的看法会形成对立和纷争。因此，庄子主张，超越自我立场，不以自己的标准去看待他者，就能够消弭事物之间的对立与是非。以这样的视角或态度去观照世界，就把握了道的关键。

Literally, this term means pivot of Dao. It first appeared in *Zhuangzi* written by the ancient Chinese philosopher Zhuangzi (369?-286 BC). It is pointed out in *Zhuangzi* that people tend to look at others from their own perspectives or standards, but such different views or standards often give rise to confrontation and disagreement. Therefore, Zhuangzi maintained that people should transcend their own views and go beyond their own standards when viewing other people or things, thus avoiding or resolving conflicts or disputes. By taking this key approach to others and things, one can gain a true understanding of Dao.

引例 Citation：

◎彼亦一是非，此亦一是非。果且有彼是乎哉？果且无彼是乎哉？彼是莫得其偶，谓之道枢。(《庄子·齐物论》)

（彼有它的是非，此也有它的是非。果真有彼此的分别吗？果真无彼此的分别吗？彼此之间不相对立，就是道的关键。）

This object has its reason for being the way it is, while the other one also has its own rationale for being the way it is. Is there truly a difference between the two? Or is there truly no difference between them? A non-confrontational approach to the two is key to understanding Dao. (*Zhuangzi*)

décāo 德操

Moral Integrity

对道德的坚守。出自《荀子·劝学》。荀子（前313？—前238）认为，人可以通过不断的学习来提高自身的道德修养。但人的德行容易受到各种外界因素的影响而有所缺失，因此荀子十分重视对德行的坚守。“德操”即是让自己的视听、言语、思虑始终符合道德礼法的要求，不被任何外在事物干扰。具备“德操”是成就完善人格的基础。

This term refers to maintaining moral integrity. It comes from the book *Xunzi*. Xunzi (313?-238 BC) believed that one could improve his moral cultivation through constant study. However, the impact of external factors could cause moral lapse. Hence Xunzi attached great importance to maintaining moral integrity. This means that one should always be guided by the norms of propriety in his thoughts, statements and acts, and should be unaffected by any external factors. Maintaining moral integrity is the basis for refining one's character.

引例 Citation：

◎是故权利不能倾也，群众不能移也，天下不能荡也。生乎由是，死乎由是，夫是之谓德操。(《荀子·劝学》)

（因此，［达到很高道德修养的人，］权力和利益不能使他倾覆，众人不能使他改变，天下任何事物不能使他动摇。活着经由它，死也经由它，这就叫作“德操”。）

Therefore, a person of high moral cultivation is not lured by power or gain. He is not swayed by others, and does not waver in the face of anything. He remains so in both life and death – this is what moral integrity means. (*Xunzi*)

déwéishànzhèng 德惟善政

The Virtue of Those Exercising Power Is Reflected in Good Governance.

执政者的德行体现为良好的施政。这是中国古代政典《尚书·大禹谟》提出的政治理念。对于执政者而言，所谓德行，并非只是个人品行的实现，更不能只是口头空谈，而必须外化或具体化为实际的施政行为与治理实效。也就是说，执政者的德行是由其努力达到的良好的治理状态来定义的，政治治理没做好，也就无从谈论执政者的美德。而良好的政治，其根本目标在于使百姓过上好的生活。这一理念是民本德政思想的凝聚与融合。

That the virtue of those exercising power is reflected in good governance is a political concept put forward in *The Book of History*, an ancient Chinese political classic. For one who exercises power, virtue is not just maintaining his moral integrity, certainly not empty talk. Rather, it must find expression in his interactions with others and effective governance. In other words, the virtue of one who exercises power is defined by good governance that he strives to achieve. If one who exercises power fails to maintain good political governance, his virtue is called into question. Ultimately, good government should deliver a good life to the people. What this concept stresses is the importance of virtuous governance for the people.

引例 Citation：

◎德惟善政，政在养民。(《尚书·大禹谟》)

(帝王的德行要体现为良好的施政，施政要以养育民众为目的。)

A ruler should manifest his virtue in good governance, and the goal of governance is to bring a good life to the people. (*The Book of History*)

diāozhuó qíngxìng, zǔzhī cílìng 雕琢情性，组织辞令

Ennoble One's Sentiment to Produce Fine Writing

陶冶提炼自己的思想情感，组织成精湛优美的文章。诗文不是词句的简

单组合，而与作者的情性相关。“情性”可以理解为人的思想情感及对自然人生的深刻感悟等。作者由个人的思想情感出发，选取合适的辞藻语句来表达，使之能传达出自己的情感与观点，进而感染或启迪更多的读者。这是因为文学作品打动人的地方，往往在于独特而深刻的情感体验与理性思考。因此，缺乏真实思想情感和深刻感悟的人，即使能组织调动很多华丽的辞藻，其作品最终只能是空洞苍白、不知所云。

A writer needs to refine his feelings and thoughts before he can produce good writing. Prose and poetry are not a crude combination of words and sentences; they are closely associated with the author's sentiment. Here, sentiment can be understood as a person's feelings and thoughts as well as his cognition of nature and life. Starting off from his own feelings and thoughts, the writer chooses appropriate wording and sentence patterns to voice his feelings and thoughts. By doing so, he aims to affect and inspire more readers. The greatest attraction of a literary work lies in the profound and unique emotional experience and rational cognition it conveys. Therefore, a writer lacking in emotion, thought and apprehension, even if he exerts his rhetorical skills to the utmost, will only produce superfluous and nonsensical things.

引例 Citations：

◎至夫子继圣，独秀前哲。镕钧“六经”，必金声而玉振；雕琢情性，组织辞令。木铎起而千里应，席珍流而万世响，写天地之辉光，晓生民之耳目矣。（刘勰《文心雕龙·原道》）

（到了孔子，继承前代的圣贤，但又超过了前人。他整理编订“六经”，如同奏乐时以钟发声、以磬收音而集圣贤思想之大成；他陶冶提炼自己的思想情感，组织成精湛优美的文章。他的教化如同木铎敲起，千里之外都会有响应；[他的道德学问] 如同座席上的珍宝，万世都会流传。他写出了天地间的光辉，启发了世人的聪明才智。）

Confucius not only inherited much from his predecessors; he also surpassed them. He compiled and edited the Six Classics in the same way a musical performance commenced with the chiming of bells and concluded with the sound of a stone chime, giving each sagely thought a place in his collections. He refined his feelings and thoughts and turned them into elegant prose. His doctrines seemed to sound like a large wooden bell, with echoes from a thousand *li* away. His virtue and learning reminded one of the treasures highly appreciated, which would be passed down from generation to generation. His writing highlighted the splendor of the natural world and inspired people's wisdom. (Liu Xie: *The Literary Mind and the Carving of Dragons*)

◎诗缘情而绮靡。（陆机《文赋》）

（诗歌源于情感因而形式华丽好看。）

Poetry, springing from emotions, reads beautifully in its form of expression. (Lu Ji: The Art of Writing)

fán cǎi guǎ qíng, wèi zhī bì yàn 繁采寡情，味之必厌

Excessive Adornment and Lack of True Feeling Make One's Writing Dull.

文章只有繁富的文采而缺乏真情实感，欣赏起来必然令人生厌。出自南朝刘勰（465？—520？或 532？）《文心雕龙・情采》。它旨在探讨情与采的关系。"情"即情感、情理，可理解为作品中的思想情感及内容；"采"即文采，可理解为文采、修饰，属于作品的形式因素。修饰过多，文采

过滥，情感和内容却单薄寡淡，这样的作品读起来必然令人生厌。“情”与“采”犹如自然界中动物的皮毛与纹样，只追求纹样美丽而损害皮毛，是非常不合理的。

This term first appeared in *The Literary Mind and the Carving of Dragons* by Liu Xie (465?-520? or 532?) of the Southern Dynasties. It focuses on the relationship between feeling and style. Here, *qing* (情) means "sensibility" or "reason-based passion," and refers to feelings, thought and content in a literary work. *Cai* (采) means "literary grace." It refers to formal beauty or literary adornment, highlighting the formal aspects of a work. Excessive adornment and lack of true feeling and content inevitably make a work boring. The relationship between feeling and style is comparable to that between an animal fur and its stripes. It would be absurd to destroy a fur for the sake of preserving its stripes.

引例 Citation:

◎言以文远，诚哉斯验。心术既形，英华乃赡。吴锦好渝，舜英徒艳。繁采寡情，味之必厌。（刘勰《文心雕龙·情采》）

（语言要讲究文采和技巧才能流传广泛久远，这的确已经得到了证验。如果懂得了如何表现情志，就可以自如展现丰富的文采。吴地出产的锦绣容易变色，木槿花只能美艳一时。只有繁富的文采而缺乏真情实感，欣赏起来必然令人生厌。）

Beautiful wording with literary grace spreads far and wide. This has been proved sufficiently true. Once we know how to express our feelings and aspirations, we will be able to display our literary talent with ease. The brocades from the Wu area easily lose their splendor. Hibiscus flowers endure only for a short time. If intricate rhetoric lacks true feeling, it will soon lose its appeal. (Liu Xie: *The Literary Mind and the Carving of Dragons*)

fēiyuè 非乐

Oppose and Ban Music

反对、禁止音乐。它是墨子（前 468？ —前 376）的主要思想之一。墨子认为应当为天下兴利除害，凡是有利于国家和人民的就提倡，不利于国家和人民的就禁止。针对当时儒家所提倡的以礼乐治理天下的思想与统治阶级耽于声色、疏于治政的弊端，墨子将音乐视为天下之大害。墨子认为，制造乐器势必搜敛财物，制成的乐器又不能为人民所用，无法解决人民真正的疾苦。音乐还耽误正常的生产活动，人们一旦沉迷于音乐，往往就会荒废自己的本业。综合这些原因，墨子提出应当禁止音乐。墨子从社会功利的层面来批判音乐并反对儒家的乐教，有一定的合理性，但同时也有矫枉过正的一面。

This term is basic to the thinking of Mozi (468?-376 BC), in whose view a ruler should promote all that is beneficial, and eliminate all that is harmful. He stood in opposition to the Confucian idea of ruling a country through ritual propriety, and held that the ruling class' abandonment to pleasure and neglect of state business was bringing great harm to society. According to him, the manufacture of musical instruments involves extracting much wealth from ordinary people, yet instruments thus produced cannot be used by them or serve to relieve their suffering. Music itself also hinders normal productive activities, as once people become obsessed with music, they may ignore their proper duties. Therefore, Mozi proposed that music should be banned. From the perspective of societal benefit, he opposed the Confucian idea of educating the masses through music. This argument is not without merit, but shows an element of over-correction.

引例 Citations：

◎姑尝厚措敛乎万民，以为大钟、鸣鼓、琴瑟、竽笙之声，以求兴天下之利，除天下之害，而无补也。是故子墨子曰："为乐非也！"（《墨子·非乐上》）

（如果用加重向民众搜敛财物的办法，用来制作巨钟、响鼓、琴瑟、竽笙等乐器，借此希望兴办对天下有利的事业，去除对天下有害的东西，是没有任何补益的。所以墨子说："兴作音乐是不好的！"）

Extracting wealth from the common folk to craft instruments such as chimes, drums, zithers and pipes serves no conceivable good, even if its original purpose is to promote the beneficial and eliminate the harmful. Therefore Mozi said: "Propagating music is pernicious!" (*Mozi*)

◎今王公大人，惟毋为乐，亏夺民之衣食之财，以拊乐如此多也。是故子墨子曰："为乐非也！"（《墨子·非乐上》）

（现在的王公大人，为了兴作音乐，夺取人民的衣食财物来用于演奏音乐，已是如此的严重。因此墨子说："兴作音乐是不好的！"）

The nobility of today have already gone too far in seizing food, clothing and other items from ordinary people for the sake of making music. Therefore Mozi said: "Propagating music is pernicious!" (*Mozi*)

fènghuáng 凤凰

Phoenix

传说中的神鸟，百鸟之王。雄的称"凤"，雌的称"凰"。秦汉以降，帝王比作“龙”，皇后及嫔妃比作“凤”，“凤凰”遂开始整体雌化，常单名“凤”。关于其种类和形象的描述历经复杂的演变过程，成为多种鸟兽特征组合成的神物。如郭璞《尔雅注》描述为：“鸡头、燕颔、蛇颈、龟背、鱼尾，五彩色，高六尺许。”“凤凰”最早应当是原始部落图腾，后被当作太平盛世的征兆，还用于对美满姻缘的祝福，含有高贵、和谐、吉祥、幸福等意。它与“龙”一样，是中华民族的一个重要文化符号。

Fenghuang (凤凰 phoenix) is a legendary divine bird and the king of all birds. *Feng* (凤) is male, and *huang* (凰) is female. Beginning in the Qin and Han dynasties, emperors were referred to as *long* (龙dragons) while queens and royal concubines were called *feng* (凤phoenix), so *fenghuang* came to mean women only. The description of the phoenix as a species and its image changed over the centuries, eventually making it a divine bird with both bird and animal features. For example, in Guo Pu's *Commentaries on Er Ya*, the phoenix is described as “a colorful six-*chi*-tall bird with a chicken's head, a swallow's jaw, a snake's neck, a turtle's back, and a fish's tail.” In the very early days, the phoenix was probably just a primitive tribal totem. Later, however, it became a symbol of peace and prosperity. It was also used to bless marriages, as it represents nobleness, harmony, auspiciousness, and happiness. Like the dragon, the phoenix is an important cultural symbol of the Chinese nation.

引例 Citations：

◎诗曰：“凤凰秋秋，其翼若干（gān），其声若箫，有凤有凰，乐帝之心。”此不蔽之福也。（《荀子·解蔽》）

（诗云：“凤凰翩翩起舞，羽翼似盾一样雄壮，鸣声似箫一样动听，又有凤来又有凰，帝王心中喜洋洋。”这是认识没受到遮蔽而带来的幸福啊！）

It is said in an ancient poem: "When the phoenixes dance, their wings are as strong as shields, and they sing as beautifully as melody from a vertical bamboo flute. So the king is overjoyed by the presence of both male and female phoenixes." This is indeed a great fortune because it suggests the king remains clear-minded and has a penetrating vision. (*Xunzi*)

◎治化周浃，凤凰来仪也。（《资治通鉴·唐纪八·太宗贞观二年》）

（国家治理井然有序，民众教化普及周遍，凤凰来舞而有容仪。）

When the country is well-governed and all the people are enlightened, the phoenixes will come to dance. (*History as a Mirror*)

◎羽族之长，名为凤凰。一日失雄，三年感伤。虽有众鸟，不为匹双。（干宝《搜神记》卷十六）

（鸟类之王，名叫凤凰。一日凤死，凰久哀伤。鸟虽有很多，凰不再配对成双。）

The phoenix is the king of all birds. Once a phoenix dies, its partner cannot overcome sadness and will not mate with another, though there are many available. (Gan Bao: *Anecdotes About Spirits and Immortals*)

gōngxíng 躬行

Practice in Person

亲自践行。出自《论语·述而》。"躬"意为亲身、亲自，"行"指个人的道德修养活动。在儒家看来，要在生活实践中成就君子人格就必须身体力行。"躬行"之说蕴含着知行合一的观念。儒家反对人在现实活动中种种知行不一的行为，强调要将所认知的道德原则充分贯彻在自身的生活行动当中。

This term first appeared in *The Analects*. *Gong* (躬) means in person and *xing* (行) refers to the cultivation of morals. According to Confucianism, one should cultivate his morals in everyday life to develop personal integrity. This term embodies the view that knowledge and action should be closely integrated with each other. Confucianism is against those who fail to observe moral principles they preach themselves, emphasizing that people should always follow moral principles in their daily lives.

引例 Citation：

◎子曰："文，莫吾犹人也。躬行君子，则吾未之有得。"（《论语·述而》）

（孔子说："文献学问，我大概与别人差不多。按君子的标准亲自践行，那我还未完成。"）

Confucius said: "As far as knowledge of literature is concerned, what I've achieved is similar to that of others. But when it comes to the practice of moral principles as a man of integrity, I still have a long way to go." (*The Analects*)

guó wú yì, suī dà bì wáng 国无义，虽大必亡

A Powerful Country Without Righteousness Is Doomed to Fall.

国家如果不讲道义，那么即便强大，也必然衰亡。道义原则应当是国家建立或得以存在的正当性依据。如果背离了这一原则，只是凭借强力或武力进行统治，那么国家就成了恶的存在。这样的国家，不会得到人民的拥护，也不会获得正义国家的赞同，而它所拥有的强力或武力从根本上也会变得毫无意义，势必不能长久。它与"国以义为利"同理，与"王道"理念相通，是中华"文明"精神的又一体现。

Any country without righteousness will decline and fall, no matter how powerful it is. The principle of righteousness is the foundation or moral core for the founding and survival of a country. Deviating from this principle of righteousness and resorting to force or military might to rule will ultimately lead to a country being evil and ruinous. Such a country will not gain support from its people, nor will it be endorsed by other countries that uphold justice. Its force or military might will become useless eventually, and it will not last for long. The meaning of the term is similar to the concepts of "the kingly way" and that "a state should regard righteousness as a benefit." It is another concept that reflects the spirit of Chinese civilization.

引例 Citation：

◎国之所以存者，仁义是也；人之所以生者，行善是也。国无义，虽大必亡；人无善志，虽勇必伤。（《淮南子·主术训》）

（国家赖以存在的根基是仁义，人赖以生存的根基是行善。一个国家如果不讲道义，那么即便强大也必然衰亡；一个人如果没有了向善之心，那么即便勇猛也必定会伤及自身。）

A country relies on benevolence and righteousness for its existence, whereas an individual relies on kindness and good behavior. No matter how powerful a country may be, it is doomed to fall if devoid of righteousness. No matter how courageous an individual may be, lacking a kind and good heart he will eventually hurt himself. (*Huainanzi*)

hé'érbùliú 和而不流

Living in Harmony with Others Without Losing Moral Ground

和睦而不顺从于流俗。早期儒家的《中庸》《荀子》等文献中都提到"和而不流"的观念。儒家倡导人与人之间有序、和睦的关系。但如果一味追求与人和睦，则容易出于人情关系的考虑而丧失对道德原则的坚守，以致同流合污。因此儒家强调要在保持和睦关系的同时，始终坚守道德原则。

This concept of living in harmony with others without losing moral ground was mentioned in early Confucian classics such as *The Doctrine of the Mean* and *Xunzi*. Confucianism believed that interpersonal relations should be in proper order and harmonious. But it was concerned that if one only pursues harmony, desire to foster personal ties can easily lead to a failure to abide by the moral code and to loss of moral ground. Confucianism therefore emphasized the importance of abiding by one's moral standard while maintaining harmonious relations with others.

引例 Citations:

◎君子和而不流，强哉矫。(《礼记·中庸》)

(君子能与人和睦相处而不顺从于流俗，是刚强的表现。)

A man of virtue lives in harmony with others without losing moral ground – such is his strength. (*The Book of Rites*)

◎夫声乐之入人也深，其化人也速，故先王谨为之文。乐中平则民和而不流，乐肃庄则民齐而不乱。(《荀子·乐论》)

(音乐对人的影响很深，感化人的速度也很快，因此先王谨慎地创制乐章。

音乐中正平和，则民众和睦而不顺从于流俗；音乐肃穆庄严，则民众整齐划一而不混乱。）

Music exerts a profound impact on people and rapidly transforms them. This is why past kings were very careful when setting out rules of musical composition. If music is balanced and tranquil in tone, then people will live in harmony without losing moral ground; if music is solemn in tone, people will be in proper order and not be unruly in behavior. (*Xunzi*)

hòushēng-kěwèi 后生可畏

Young People Should Be Highly Regarded.

年轻人是可敬畏的。年轻意味着活力、创造力与无限的可能性，意味着未来和希望，他们不可限量，而且会取得超越前辈的成就。因此，长辈应以敬畏、大度之心对待、奖掖、提携后辈。这是孔子（前 551—前 479）所确立的良好的代际关系准则，一直为后世所崇尚与阐扬。后生可畏实际隐含着对新一代的期许和对未来的敬意，隐含着对于人类不断进步与美好前景的坚定信念和乐观态度。

Youth means vitality, creativity, and unlimited possibilities as well as future and hope. Young people have great potential and they will outperform their predecessors. Therefore, elders should treat, reward, and promote the younger generation with respect and an open mind. This is the norm for governing intergenerational relations established by Confucius (551–479 BC), a norm that has been observed by later generations. The view young people should be highly regarded contains hopes for the new generation and respect for the future.

It also demonstrates a firm belief and optimism in the continuous advance of humanity and its future.

引例 Citations：

◎后生可畏，焉知来者之不如今也？（《论语・子罕》）
（年轻人是可敬畏的，怎么知道他们将来赶不上现在的人呢？）

Young people should be highly regarded. How do we know that the latecomers will not catch up with us? (*The Analects*)

◎后生可畏，何代无人？（刘知几（jī）《史通・杂说下》）
（年轻人是可敬畏的，哪一代没有杰出人物呢？）

Young people should be highly regarded. Which generation does not have outstanding figures? (Liu Zhiji: *All About Historiography*)

◎后生可畏，不可总守过去也。（释普济《五灯会元・长庆藏用禅师》）
（年轻人是可敬畏的，不能总是固守从前的成就。）

Young people should be highly regarded, and we should not rest on past laurels. (Shi Puji: *A Compilation of Five Chan Masters' Writings on Buddha's Teachings*)

jiǎxiàng-jiànyì 假象见意

Use Imagery to Express Meaning

借助物象、形象的描绘含蓄表达作者的主观意旨。是古代诗文的一种创作手法。“象”指物象，可理解为一切现实存在的或虚构的事物；“意”即意旨，泛指作者的主观思想情感。它可溯源于《周易》和《诗经》：《周易》用卦象来象征各类事物、现象、事件，并表现与某类事物、现象、事件相关的认知、意愿和情感，由此派生出象征手法；《诗经》借助现实存在的或虚构的物象、场景来表达思想感情，由此派生出比兴手法。“比”是以单一之“象”比附明了的“意”，取象即可明意；“兴”是将丰富复杂的意蕴寄托于不确定的物象或场景，意象之间没有明确的对应关系，类似于象征、暗喻。“比”和“兴”虽然都运用“假象见意”的手法，但是“比”“兴”手法运用的动因或是由于难尽其意而只能含蓄，或是由于难以启齿而只能委婉；“假象见意”的动因则是要用丰富的物象来表现作者多样化的感觉、感受和感悟。“假象见意”不仅是中国古典诗歌一贯的创作手法，而且也隐含古人在创作时不甘平庸、勇于创新的精神。

This term refers to the act of borrowing physical imagery to subtly convey the author's personal message. It was a means of creating prose and poetry in ancient China. *Xiang* (象) can indicate either a physical image or more broadly any real or fictitious thing in the world. *Yi* (意) means "authorial intent" or "an author's personal feelings and thoughts." All this can be traced back to *The Book of Changes* and *The Book of Songs*. In the former, hexagrams are used to symbolize various things, phenomena and events, as well as corresponding cognition, volition and feelings, thus creating symbolic devices. In the latter, real or fictitious objects and scenery are used to express feelings, thus creating analogy and association. Analogy here involves the use of a single image to show an explicit message; to adopt an image is to convey a message. Association, however, embeds an intricate and nuanced message in less defined objects and scenery; in this case there is no clear correspondence between an image and a message. In a sense, association can be likened to symbolism or metaphor. Although analogy and association, too, use imagery to convey meaning, they do so either because the author must be ambiguous if he wants to fully express himself or because he must be indirect in order to avoid embarrassment. The use of imagery to express meaning, on the other hand, aims to reveal wide-ranging sensations, feelings and sudden enlightenment through a rich reserve of imagery. It has remained a constant means of creating classic Chinese poetry, but it also indicates the refusal of ancient Chinese poets to be mediocre and their daring to be innovative.

引例 Citations：

◎江则假象见意，班则貌题直书 。（释皎然《诗式·团扇二篇》）

（江淹的《班婕妤咏扇》是借班婕妤团扇上所绘的意象而表达主观意旨，而班婕妤的原诗是直接以团扇自身形象为题叙写情思。）

"An Ode to the Moon-shaped Fan" by Jiang Yan conveys the poet's personal message through the image painted by Ban Jieyu on a moon-shaped fan, whereas Ban Jieyu's original poem expresses her feelings directly through that fan as an image. (Shi Jiaoran: *Poetic Styles*)

◎取象曰比，取义曰兴，义即象下之意。（释皎然《诗式·用事》）

（从事物的外部形象方面着眼是"比"，从事物的内在意蕴方面着眼是"兴"，而意蕴就含在形象之中。）

Analogy means comparing the appearances of things, while association means grasping the essence of things. Meaning is what underlies the appearance. (Shi Jiaoran: *Poetic Styles*)

jiànxíng 践形

Cultivate One's Innate Quality to Be Revealed in One's Appearance

实现形貌之中的本性。出自《孟子·尽心上》。孟子（前372？—前289）认为，人的形体、样貌是天生所具的，包含着天赋的本性。但人们往往空有其表，而无法充分体现其本性。只有圣人能够体察并发挥人的天性，并使之体现于外在的形体、样貌，从而充分发挥形貌的功用。

This means one's innate quality can be cultivated and shown through one's appearance. It originated in the Chinese classic *Mencius*. Mencius (372?-289 BC), an ancient Chinese thinker, believed that a person's physical appearance embodies his innate quality. However, the physical appearance of many people fails to give expression to their innate quality. Only a sage can see and make use of such quality and demonstrate it through physical appearance, enabling the physical appearance to perform its due function.

引例 Citations:

◎孟子曰："形色，天性也；惟圣人然后可以践形。"（《孟子·尽心上》）

（孟子说："人的形体、样貌，是天生的本性。只有圣人能够实现形貌之中的本性。"）

Mencius said: "A person's physical features and appearance can tell a lot about one's innate quality. Only a sage can demonstrate such quality through his physique and appearance." (*Mencius*)

◎践形，人有形，形必有性。耳，形也，必尽其聪，然后能践耳之形；目，形也，必尽其明，然后能践目之形。（《朱子语类》卷六十）

（践形，是说人有其形体，形体必有其本性。耳朵，是人的形体，必然要竭尽听闻之聪慧，然后才能实现耳朵的本性。眼睛，是人的形体，必然要竭尽目视之明晰，然后才能实现眼睛的本性。）

When I talk about expression of innate quality through appearance and manner, I mean that people's physical appearance reveals their innate quality. An ear is a part of one's physical appearance; it can only function when it can hear as well as it should. The same applies to eyes: they can only function when they can see as far and clearly as they should. (Categorized *Conversations of Master Zhu Xi*)

jiāngshānzhīzhù 江山之助

Inspiration from Mountains and Rivers

江河山岳的景致启发、助益了文人的创作灵感和文学构思。"江山"指江河山岳，它与"庙堂"相对，多与隐逸相关。中国古代文人如果不能得志于庙堂，或者有意逃离庸俗琐碎的功名利禄，则往往放旷于山水之间。山水是诗歌、文章的描写对象，也是文人情感的寄托。山水诗在晋宋之时兴起。山水成为独立的审美对象，从山水中获得的灵感与领悟，有助于丰富文学作品的审美样态。"江山之助"所助的不仅是文学作品中对山水景物的描写，更有助于文人精神世界的陶冶和提升，使其获得更超越的视野和胸襟，在整体的文学体验和文学表达方面可以达到更高的境界。

Mountains and rivers often inspire the literati in their literary conception. They use such landscapes in contrast to the imperial court. Thus, mountains and rivers symbolize a reclusive way of life. When ancient men of letters were unappreciated by the bureaucracy or when they wanted to escape from mundane duties and the crass pursuit of position and wealth, they might find their own meaning among mountains and rivers. They were not only the objects of poetic and prosaic description, but also where men of letters sought spiritual consolation. Mountain-and-river poetry first emerged between the Jin Dynasty and Song of the Southern Dynasties. Mountains and rivers became independent objects of artistic appreciation. Inspiration thus drawn adds to the aesthetic diversity of literary expression. The sight of mountains and rivers not only aids actual description of natural scenery in literary works, but also helps to chasten and elevate men of letters' spiritual world, expand their horizons and broaden their minds. Such aesthetic activities raise them to greater heights in literary experience and expression.

引例 Citations：

◎若乃山林皋壤，实文思之奥府。略语则阙，详说则繁。然屈平所以能洞监《风》《骚》之情者，抑亦江山之助乎？（刘勰《文心雕龙·物色》）

（至于山林原野，确实是启发文思灵感的宝库。叙写简略就会缺漏，描述详细又显烦琐。然而屈原能够深切体察《国风》和骚赋的情韵，大概也是得到了山川景物的帮助吧？）

As for forested mountains and the vast countryside, they are indeed a fertile source of literary inspiration. Brevity can result in too many omissions whereas thoroughness may seem trivial. However, Qu Yuan was able to appreciate the charm of "Ballads from the States" and works in the *Sao* Style (Flowery Style), most probably because he was aided by the sight of mountains and rivers. (Liu Xie: *The Literary Mind and the Carving of Dragons*)

◎物色相召，江山助人。请振翰林，用濡笔海云尔。（骆宾王《初秋登司马楼宴诗》）

（风物景致召唤人，山山水水帮助人。请有才华的人振奋起来，饱蘸笔墨尽情为文吧。）

With the scenery so inspiringly beautiful and the landscape so exhilarating, talented men should really cheer up and set brush to paper. (Luo Binwang: Improvising a Poem While Attending a Banquet at the Marshal's Home on an Early Autumn Day)

jiàng zài wài, jūn mìng yǒu suǒ bù shòu 将在外，君命有所不受

A General Out in the Battlefield Can Choose Not to Obey the King's Order.

将军在外领兵打仗，君主的命令有的可以不服从。这是历代公认的处理战时君权与军权、君命与将令关系的基本原则。其理由主要有三：其一，打仗是很专业的事情，君主未必精通；其二，君主不在前线，对实际情况未必了解；其三，双方有空间距离，信息传达不及时，而战况却瞬息万变，战机稍纵即逝。其要义在于充分尊重前线指挥官的临机处置权，争取作战胜利，有利于国家。

The term means that a military general who is leading his soldiers fighting enemy in a faraway place has the right not to heed the orders from the king. That saying is historically acknowledged as a basic principle for balancing powers between the king and the military commander, and between an order from the king and one from a general. The reasons are threefold. First, warfare requires unique skills, and the king may not have the expertise. Second, the king who is not on the frontline may not know the situation of the battle. Third, the spatial distance between the king and the general makes it impossible for a timely communication of information. In addition, the situation on the battlefield is constantly changing. Any hesitation or delay in decision-making might risk losing an opportunity for victory. The point of this principle is to give frontline commanders sufficient discretion for the sake of winning victory for the benefit of the country.

引例 Citations:

◎途有所不由，军有所不击，城有所不攻，地有所不争，君命有所不受。（《孙子·九变》）

（道路有的可以不走，敌军有的可以不打，城池有的可以不攻，有的地方可以不争，君主的命令有的可以不听。）

There are times when we do not have to take certain roads, engage certain enemy troops, attack certain cities and towns, fight over certain places, or follow certain orders from the king. (*The Art of War*)

◎将在外，主令有所不受，以便国家。（《史记·魏公子列传》）

（将军在外领兵打仗，君主的命令有的可以不服从，这是为了利于国家。）

A general out in the battlefield leading soldiers fighting can choose not to follow the king's certain orders. That is for the benefit of the country. (*Records of the Historian*)

◎大将专征，君命有所不受。临敌制变，安可预谋？（《百战奇略·变战》）

（大将主持征战，君主的命令有的可以不服从。临敌作战需要随机应变，怎么可能都预先谋划好呢？）

When a general is in charge of a military campaign, he can ignore some of the orders from the king. Situation in the battleground demands flexibility and responsiveness. How can everything be well planned out beforehand? (*Extraordinary Strategies for Various Types of Battles*)

jiàoxué-wéixiān 教学为先

Education Must Be Placed First.

教育要放在首位。这里的“先”，既表示其重要性，也表示其先行性。归纳古人相关论说，其蕴含的意思主要是：个人的成长成才；良好社会风尚的形成；国家的建设及有效治理；发现事物固有原理，发挥其固有属性，成就事功等，均离不开教育。因此，兴办教育是国家重要职能之一。这是中华民族自古及今的共识。

Here “first” expresses both the importance and priority of education. A summary of ancient works on this subject argued that education’s meanings include: nurturing individuals and their talents; forming good social mores; developing the country and its effective governance; discovering the inherent principles of things and making full use of their attributes in order to fulfill tasks – these are all inseparable from education. Therefore the promotion of education is one of the important functions of the state. This has been a consensus of the Chinese people, both past and present.

引例 Citations:

◎君子如欲化民成俗，其必由学乎！玉不琢，不成器；人不学，不知道。是故古之王者建国君民，教学为先。(《礼记·学记》)

（君子如果想要教化百姓，形成良好的社会风尚，一定要从教育入手吧！玉不雕琢，就不能成为器物；人不学习，就不会明白道理。所以古代君王建立国家、治理百姓，都把教育放在首位。）

If a man of virtue wishes to enlighten the people and establish good social mores, he must start with education. If jade is not carved, it cannot become an artistic implement; if a person does not learn, he cannot understand principles. That is why the ancient sage-kings put education first when they established their states and governed their people. (*The Book of Rites*)

◎古者建国，教学为先，所以道（dǎo）世治性，为时养器也。（《三国志·吴书·孙休传》）

（古代圣王建立国家，将教育放在首位，用它来引导世人修养品性，为当世培养所需的人才。）

When the ancient sage-kings established their states, they gave education the highest priority in order to guide the people to cultivate character, and nurture the talent needed by the times. (*The History of the Three Kingdoms*)

◎自古开物成务，必以教学为先。（《南齐书·崔祖思传》）

（自古以来，揭示万物真相，确定做事原则，就必须首先兴办教育。）

Since ancient times, education had been given the foremost priority in order to reveal the true nature of all things and to determine the principles of action. (*The History of Qi of the Southern Dynasties*)

jiéyòng 节用

Economy

节省用度。“节用”是对待物质财货的一种态度，即节约使用财货，减少不必要的财货消耗。“节用”常特指为政者不滥用自己所掌握的权力攫取民财，以满足自己的需求或行铺张浪费之事。为政者的“节用”体现着对百姓的关爱。儒家、墨家等不同学派都有“节用”的主张，但对于节省的标准和尺度，各家有着不同的认识。

Jieyong (节用) means economy, or frugality of usage. *Jieyong* is an attitude regarding material property; that is, using property sparingly and reducing its unnecessary consumption. This term was often used to point out that those in government should not abuse the powers of their office to seize wealth from the people to meet their own needs or for extravagances. *Jieyong* in those who govern is a manifestation of their care and concern for their people. Different schools of thought like the Confucians and the Mohists all advocated *jieyong*, but they had different views about its criteria and scope.

引例 Citations：

◎子曰：“道（dǎo）千乘（shèng）之国，敬事而信，节用而爱人，使民以时。”（《论语·学而》）

（孔子说：“治理有千辆兵车的大国，要严肃对待政事而有信用，节省用度而关爱百姓，役使民众要遵循农时的安排。”）

Confucius said, “When governing a powerful state which is a thousand chariots strong, one must be dedicated and trustworthy, act economically, show love for others, and have the people serve their corvée during the right seasons.” (*The Analects*)

◎是故古者圣王制为节用之法，曰：凡天下群百工，轮、车、鞼（guì）、匏、陶、冶、梓匠，使各从事其所能。曰：凡足以奉给民用，则止。诸加费不加于民利者，圣王弗为。（《墨子·节用中》）

（因此古时候的圣王制定了节用的原则：凡是天下各行的工匠，造车轮的、造车的、制作皮革的、烧制陶器的、冶炼金属的、打造木质器具的，使他们各自从事自己所擅长的工作。凡是足以供给民众使用了，就可以了。那些增加耗费而不增加民众利益的事情，圣王都不会去做。）

Therefore the ancient sage-kings laid out the principles of economy as follows. For all the craftsmen in the land, whether they be wheelwrights or carriage-builders, whether they be tanners or potters, whether they work with metal or wood – let them all make the best use of their skills. Stop once they have made enough to meet the needs of the people. Sage-kings do not do things which increase expenditures without bringing added benefits to the people. (*Mozi*)

jīnxiàng-yùzhì 金相玉质

The Look of Gold and the Texture of Jade

像黄金一样的外表、美玉一样的质地，比喻从外表到品质都非常优美。“金相玉质”既可用来形容一个人才华出众、品格优良，也可用来形容诗文作品语言华丽、思想内容丰美。“金相玉质”的人，为人群中的佼佼者；“金相玉质”的诗文，是文学作品中的上品。

This metaphor is used to describe anybody or anything that is very beautiful both internally and externally. It applies to an intellectually brilliant and morally upright person, or to a piece of prose or poetry beautiful in wording and rich in thought. A person with the look of gold and the texture of jade is a truly exceptional character. Prose and poetry comparable to gold and jade are literary works of the highest class.

引例 Citations：

◎屈原之词，诚博远矣。自终没以来，名儒博达之士著造词赋，莫不拟则其

仪表，祖式其模范，取其要妙，窃其华藻。所谓金相玉质，百世无匹，名垂罔极，永不刊灭者矣。（王逸《离骚叙》）

（屈原的作品，确实广博深远。自从他去世以后，有名的儒者和博学通达的人创作词赋，没有人不模拟他的文学风格，遵奉他的文章体制，吸收他的精深微妙，窃用他的华美辞藻。屈原的作品，就是所说的金相玉质，百代没有匹敌，名声流传没有止境，永远不会泯灭。）

Works by Qu Yuan indeed had both breadth and depth. Since his death, famed Confucian scholars and other erudite men have all been emulating his style of writing when creating verse. They all follow the structure or layout of his writing, absorb the quintessence of his work, and steal flowery wording from him. Qu Yuan's works indeed have the look of gold and the texture of jade, unsurpassed all through the ages with fame far and wide. It will forever remain indelible in people's memory. (Wang Yi: A Preface to *Li Sao*)

◎若刀笔之中而得志行，是则金相玉质，内外俱美，实为人宝也。（《周书・苏绰传》）

（如果掌管文案的官吏又有突出的志向操行，这样的人就是金相玉质，里外都美，实在是人中的瑰宝。）

If a person in charge of official documents displays outstanding aspiration and virtue, he is assuredly endowed with the look of gold and the texture of jade, a man of fine appearance and character. Such a man is a valuable asset, indeed! (*The History of Zhou of the Northern Dynasties*)

jīngdiǎn 经典

Classics

本义为普遍的道理及记载普遍道理的文本，后泛指可作为典范的典籍。“经”本义指织布机上的经线（纵线），因经线确定后才能穿插纬线而成为织品，故引申指恒常的准则，后人将蕴含恒常道理，可奉为思想、行为准则的典籍尊之为“经”，如“六经”、佛经、《道德经》、《黄帝内经》等；“典”字本义是手捧简册（祭告神灵），引申指一切可作为标准、规范的简册、文献、书籍，进而引申出“规范、典则、常道”等义。“经典”连用，即指蕴含普遍道理的典范性、权威性著作。而在中国古代，所谓“经典”，实际主要指儒家的“四书”“五经”。近代以降，该词与英文 classics 对译，转指各领域具有典范性、权威性的经久不衰的作品，是人类精神文明的结晶。

Originally, this term referred to universal ways and the texts in which they are recorded. Later, it came to refer to written texts that set standards. *Jing* (经) here describes the warp yarns on a loom. Because warp yarns have to be steady for the weft to go through and thus create a woven fabric, it has come to signify underlying norms. Subsequently, people refer to those texts that contain underlying rules and can serve as guidelines for thought and behavior as *jing* (classics). Examples of such classics include the Six Classics, Buddhist sutras, *Laozi*, and *Yellow Emperor's Internal Canon of Medicine*. *Dian* (典) originally described the holding, with both hands, of a book of bound bamboo strips to worship the spirits. It subsequently came to include all bamboo strips, documents, and books that set standards and norms as well as such concepts as models, principles, or the constant way. Used together, those two Chinese characters refer to authoritative writings that articulate universal ways. In ancient China, this term mainly referred to the Four Books and Five Classics of Confucianism. In modern times, it has become the equivalent to the English word "classics," referring in general to authoritative writings with enduring influence in various disciplines, writings that have become a source of inspiration of human civilization.

引例 Citations:

◎经者，道之常也。（赵蕤《长短经・定名》）

（经就是［人们都应该遵循的］普遍的道理。）

Classics represent the universal way that all should follow. (Zhao Rui: *On the Thoughts of Strategists*)

◎经者，先圣之至言，仲尼之所发明，皆天人之极致，诚万代不刊之典也。（《旧唐书・薛戎传弟放》）

（经是古代圣人讲述的最普遍的道理，这些道理是孔子发现并阐明的，所揭示的都是天人之间最为精妙深远的关系，诚然是万世不能更改的普遍原理。）

Classics are universal ways mentioned by ancient sages which are discovered and articulated by Confucius. They reveal the most profound relationships between people and nature and contain universal ways that have remained true throughout generations. (*The Old Tang History*)

◎自圣贤述作，是曰经典，句皆《韶》《夏》。（刘知几（jī）《史通・叙事》）

（自从有了圣贤的著述，因此就有了"经典"，其中每句话都像舜时的《韶》乐和大禹时的《夏》乐一样感动人心。）

The writings and narrations of the sages have become classics. Every sentence in those classics is as moving as the "Shao" music in the reign of Shun or the "Xia" music in the reign of Yu. (Liu Zhiji: *All About Historiography*)

jīngwù-bājí, xīnyóu-wànrèn 精骛八极，心游万仞

Roaming Remote Realms and Soaring to Great Heights

精神奔驰于八方极远之地，心灵飞翔至万仞极高之境。是西晋陆机（261—303）对创作心理的一种形象化描述，指作家在进行艺术构思、艺术创作时，思想纵横驰骋而不受时空的限制，就像骏马驰骋于天地四方，又像心灵畅游于万仞天空。陆机指出，作家在构思之初，全部感知官能向内收缩，摒除一切杂念，保持对审美对象的高度关注，这样才能充分地激活作家的灵感，使神思上下纵横，跨越时空，无所不至，从而创作出富有审美想象力的艺术形象。

This term means that when writing, a writer should allow his mind to roam freely across the vast universe. It was first put forward by Lu Ji (261-303) when describing the thought process governing artistic creation. Lu Ji believes that in conceiving and creating a work of art, an artist should transcend both time and space, like a steed racing to all quarters of the universe or a soul soaring across the skies. When engaging in a creative activity, a writer should turn all his perceptual faculties inward, abandon any distracting thought and focus on the object of his aesthetic contemplation. Thus inspired, the writer will wander off as far as his mind allows, be unconstrained by the limits of time and space, and produce artistic images imbued with imagination.

引例 Citations：

◎赋家之心，苞括宇宙，总览人物，斯乃得之于内，不可得而传。（葛洪《西京杂记》卷二）

（辞赋作家，其内心可以囊括天地宇宙，可以纵观古今人物，这都是从他自身的修养中得到的，不可能拿来传授他人。）

A great writer can embrace all things in the world and view all historical figures in perspective. This is attributable to his self-cultivation, something he cannot simply pass on to others. (Ge Hong: *Collection of Miscellaneous Stories in the Western Capital*)

◎其始也，皆收视反听，耽思傍讯。精骛八极，心游万仞。（陆机《文赋》）

（在开始写文章时，必须停止一切视听活动，凝聚心神，广为求索，精神奔驰于八方极远之地，心灵飞翔至万仞极高之境。）

When starting to write an essay, the writer should be free from external sounds and sights and keep his mind focused, and this will allow his thoughts to roam freely across the universe. (Lu Ji: The Art of Writing)

◎文之思也，其神远矣。故寂然凝虑，思接千载。悄焉动容，视通万里。（刘勰《文心雕龙·神思》）

（文章写作时的想象和思绪，其神奇是可以超越时空的呀！所以当作家默默地凝神思考时，可以联想起千年之前的事情；他的表情微动之际，似乎看见了万里之外的情景。）

When writing, the writer may transcend time and space. When he quietly ponders, he may wander off and reach events that occurred a thousand years ago. Even a slight change in his facial expression suggests the writer may have seen, in his mind's eye, things in the far distance. (Liu Xie: *The Literary Mind and the Carving of Dragons*)

jìng 敬

Respect

恭敬，敬重。“敬”是儒家所倡导的一种美德，要求人们在对待特定的人或事物时保持恭敬、敬重的态度，如下位者对上位者、年幼者对年长者等。在不同的关系中，“敬”或侧重于敬畏之义，或更多地包含敬爱之情。“敬”体现着礼法对于人和他者关系的定位与规范。人也通过保持“敬”的态度，获得内在意识的觉醒，实现对自我的检省与约束。

This term means to treat people and things with reverence. Respect is a virtue expounded by Confucian scholars which requires people to maintain a reverential attitude towards a particular group of people or things. For example, those in a lower position should respect their superiors, and the young should respect elders. In the context of different relationships, respect means either respectful awe or respectful love. Respect is a concrete expression of rules governing interpersonal relations laid out by norms of propriety. By maintaining a respectful attitude, a person can appreciate one's inherent meaning, awaken one's inner consciousness and maintain both self-reflection and self-control.

引例 Citations：

◎樊迟问仁。子曰：“居处恭，执事敬，与人忠。虽之夷狄，不可弃也。”（《论语·子路》）

（樊迟问孔子什么是仁。孔子说：“平时要端庄，办事要恭敬，与人交往要真诚。即便到了华夏以外的地方，也不能丢弃这些原则。”）

Fan Chi asked the meaning of *ren* (benevolence). Confucius said, “Behave properly in your daily life, act with care and respect in dealing with others, and treat people with sincerity. You must not fail to do so even when you are in other countries." (*The Analects*)

◎君子敬以直内，义以方外。(《周易·文言》)

（君子通过敬的修养方式使内心正直，通过合乎义的方式使行事端方。）

A man of virtue maintains integrity by being respectful and acts properly by being upright. (*The Book of Changes*)

jūluán-bǔnà 拘挛补衲

Florid Prose and Stilted Writing

诗文不是用自己的话语直抒胸臆，而是刻意搬用典故、陈言，使作品拘谨局促而不自然、支离破碎而非浑然一体。“拘挛”指刻意、生硬用典而导致的行文拘束；“补衲”指用典过多，不能与作者自己的话语、风格融为一体，如同用碎布缝补衲衣。钟嵘（？—518？）用这一具象化的术语，生动展现出有些诗文作者过于喜好用事用典而自缚手足的形象，表明了诗文创作应当以直抒胸臆为贵。由此又延伸出如何活用前人之语和如何化用前人之意的问题。钟嵘还认为，很多作者在思想和文辞创新方面缺乏才华，只好以学问弥补这方面的不足，也有一定的合理性。

This expression is used to describe prose and poetry lacking fluency because they fail to express their authors' feelings freely, and instead borrow hackneyed allusions or phrases. Such writing is seen to lack flair, and comes across as unnatural and fragmentary. *Juluan* (拘挛) points to the lack of fluency as a result of artificial, rigid use of allusions. *Buna* (补衲) describes a failure to use appropriate allusions, often too many and out of keeping with the author's own tone and style, leaving the writing like "a garment patched together with rags." Zhong Rong (?-518?), using this term with its concrete image, vividly laid bare how some essayists and poets stifled their own works by alluding to a profusion of events and tales. He argued that prose and poetry should prize free expression of one's feelings. This yields the questions of how to borrow one's predecessors' words flexibly and how to borrow from one's predecessors' messages creatively. In Zhong's view, since many writers lack intellectual and literary talent, they understandably fall back on scholarly knowledge to make up for this inadequacy.

引例 Citations：

◎遂乃句无虚语，语无虚字，拘挛补衲，蠹文已甚。（钟嵘《诗品》卷中）

（于是没有不用典故的句子，没有无来历的字词；典故与自己的文字勉强牵合拼贴，对作品破坏严重。）

And so, all sentences must contain allusions, and every word and expression has to be traceable to some sources. Allusions are clumsily tacked onto the authors' own words, severely damaging their works. (Zhong Rong: *The Critique of Poetry*)

◎后生不知法度，描染细巧，以媚俗眼，此是人物景致便成补衲，非山水也。（李澄叟《画山水诀》）

（有些年轻画者不懂山水画的法度，将山水画上的人物景致描画、点染得非常细致精巧，以取悦世俗的审美眼光，画上的人物景致都是缝补拼合而成的，不是真正的山水画。）

Some young painters know little about rules that govern landscape painting. They depict and polish human images and scenery in a landscape painting in minute detail to appeal to plebeian tastes. Human images and scenery are all patched together; such works are not true landscape paintings. (Li Chengsou: *Gists of Landscape Painting*)

lèi 类

Category

种类，类别。“类”是对具有相同属性、特征的人或事物的指称。“类”体现着对事物共性以及不同类别事物间区别的把握。明确个体事物的类别归属，明确不同属类的区别与界限，是对事物进行命名并进而构建万物秩序的基础。古代诸多学派都对“类”的概念进行过探讨，对类名的使用、分类原则、同类事物间的关系等问题提出了各自不同的看法。

Lei (类) is used to refer to people or things which have similar attributes or characteristics. It represents recognition of the commonalities of things and the differences between categories. Establishing which categories individual entities belong to, and what distinctions and boundaries there are between different types is the basis for naming and developing an order of all things in the world. Many ancient schools of thought studied the concept of *lei*, and offered different views on the use of category names, the principles of categorization, and the relationships between objects in the same category.

引例 Citations：

◎方以类聚，物以群分，吉凶生矣。（《周易・系辞上》）

（各种方法规则按照门类汇聚，各种事物按照群属相区分，吉凶就由此产生了。）

Methods fall into categories, and entities are divided into groups. Thus good and bad appear. (*The Book of Changes*)

◎命之马，类也。若实也者必以是名也。(《墨子·经说上》)

(命名为“马”，是一个类名。只要有其实物就必然要以相应的名来指称。)

When you call something a “horse,” that is a category. If something exists, it must be called by an appropriate name. (*Mozi*)

lèizú-biànwù 类族辨物

Discerning Things Through Classification

通过分别事物的族类来辨察事物的同异。这一术语源自《周易·象上》。《周易》认为，天地万物以族类相聚合，同类的事物会聚集在一起。不同的群体之间就会显示出事物的差异。因此可以通过对聚合的群体进行区别、分类，以此来辨别事物的同异。同时也警醒人们，应谨慎选择自己所亲近的群体，要与君子同群。

This term means to ascertain the similarities and differences between things by classifying them. This phrase originated in *The Book of Changes*, which regarded everything in the world as belonging to different categories, and those with similar features being in the same group. Thus, one can tell the similarities and differences of things by grouping those that have common features. This concept also alerts people that they should be careful in interacting with people and should stick to like-minded people and those with moral integrity.

引例 Citation：

◎天与火，同人。君子以类族辨物。(《周易·象上》)

（上卦为乾象天，下卦为离象火，是同人卦。君子通过分别事物的族类来辨察事物的同异。）

The upper trigram is *qian*, which is the image of heaven. The lower trigram is *li*, which is the image of fire. These form the hexagram for "fellowship." A man of virtue discerns similarities and differences in things based on how they are classified. (*The Book of Changes*)

miàozào-zìrán 妙造自然

Perfect Naturalness

作品臻于自然天成的妙境。是由晚唐诗人司空图（837—908）提出的诗学批评术语。这一观念源于道家崇尚自然的美学观，堪称中国文艺理论的精髓。司空图以“妙造自然”作为审美理想与追求，并将“自然”列为诗歌的二十四种风格之一。“妙造自然”既是诗人所创造的一种自然美的境界，也是诗人在诗歌创作中对自然美的自觉追求。“妙造”二字，与西方美学传统的“摹仿”理论形成了鲜明对比，强调了艺术家与自然万物生命既有同一性又有超越自然万物生命的主体创造精神。

This term describes a poetic work which has attained the sublime state of natural appeal. First put forward by late-Tang poet Sikong Tu (837-908) as a term of poetry discourse, it originates from the nature-revering aesthetic of Daoism and embodies a fundamental tenet of the theory of Chinese art. Sikong Tu championed the aesthetic principle of perfect naturalness and listed it as one of the twenty-four styles of poetry. Perfect naturalness is an ideal natural state of beauty created by poets, and also a conscious exertion sought by them in poetic composition. This notion stands in contrast to the imitation theory in Western aesthetic tradition. It seeks to achieve oneness between the poet and all lives in the universe, and at the same time maintains the individual creativity above all other lives.

引例 Citations：

◎生气远出，不著死灰。妙造自然，伊谁与裁？（司空图《二十四诗品·精神》）

（作品生气活力超然远出，绝无丝毫刻板死灰。已是臻于自然天成的妙境，谁还能够加以剪裁？）

A poetic work that is free from banality and exudes vigor reaches a state of perfect naturalness beyond any improvement. (Sikong Tu: Twenty-four Styles of Poetry)

◎夫画道之中，水墨最为上。肇自然之性，成造化之功。（王维《画学秘诀》）

（在绘画技法中，水墨山水最为上乘。它肇始于自然的本性，展现天地万物创生变化之功。）

Of all painting techniques, ink landscape is of the highest order. It portrays the features of nature and describes the life and change of all things in the world. (Wang Wei: Gists of Painting)

◎凝神遐想，妙悟自然，物我两忘，离形去智。（张彦远《历代名画记》卷二）

（凝聚心神，自由畅想，对自然之美的体悟达到绝妙境地，忘记了外在世界，也忘记了自身，脱离形体的束缚，抛弃知识的局限。）

By keeping his mind focused and giving free rein to his thoughts, the artist can reach such a fascinating state in appreciating the beauty of nature as to become oblivious to the external world and his own self, free from the fetters of physical forms and limitations of knowledge. (Zhang Yanyuan: *Famous Paintings Through History*)

mínshēng 民生

Livelihood of the People

百姓的生计或生活。百姓为了谋生，往往不辞辛劳。为政者对此应予体恤，提供必要的生存条件以及政策、制度保障，而不可侵扰、危害民生。这是治国理政、实现社会长治久安的基本前提。如果百姓生活困顿，衣食无着，就会有人铤而走险，这对执政者来说也不是好事情。"安民"的根本在于重视并解决好民生问题。

The term means life or livelihood of the people. Earning a living is often hard. Rulers should show empathy, provide necessary conditions for survival, and draw up suitable policies and systems. They should not bully or harm the people. Good state governance as well as lasting social peace and stability are dependent on this. If life is too harsh and people lack food and shelter, there will be desperation and unrest which will not benefit the rulers either. Providing a decent livelihood is the key to a peaceful and contented populace.

引例 Citations：

◎民生在勤，勤则不匮。(《左传·宣公十二年》)

（百姓的生计在于勤劳，勤劳就不会匮乏。）

People's livelihood comes from hard work, which in turn ensures no scarcity. (*Zuo's Commentary on The Spring and Autumn Annals*)

◎内治缺而后戎马生，民生促而后盗贼起。（计六奇《明季北略·卷十八·吴履中论二失》）

（国内治政有缺失，天下就会发生战事；百姓生活窘迫，盗贼就会兴起。）

Failings in domestic governance lead to war; widespread poverty abets the rise of thieves and bandits. (Ji Liuqi: *Local Historical Accounts from the North of the Late Ming Dynasty*)

◎上天厚民生，则赋敛宜缓。（黄宗羲《明儒学案·蕺（jí）山学案·忠端刘念台先生宗周》）

（上天体恤百姓生活，所以执政者向百姓征收赋税应该宽缓。）

Heaven commiserates with the lives of the people, so rulers should impose lighter taxes. (Huang Zongxi: *Commentaries on Writings of Famous Scholars of the Ming Dynasty*)

nèixǐng 内省

Introspection

自我省察。“内省”是儒家所主张的一种道德修养方式。儒家认为，道德的养成固然需要言行符合外在的道德规范，但在根本上取决于内在道德意识的确立。因此，在关注人的言行举止的同时，儒家更重视内心的修养，主张通过不断省察自己真实的用心，确立并持守内在的道德意识。

This term, *neixing* (内省), means introspection, or self-examination.

Introspection was a form of moral cultivation advocated by the Confucians. They felt that while moral cultivation certainly required words and deeds to adhere externally to moral standards, it was fundamentally dependent on the internal formation of moral awareness. Hence, while they were concerned with people's words and deeds, they placed even more emphasis on cultivation of the inner self. They favored constant examination of one's true intentions, as well as the formation and observance of internal moral awareness.

引例 Citation：

◎子曰："内省不疚，夫何忧何惧？"（《论语·颜渊》）

（孔子说："自我省察而没有愧疚之处，有什么可担忧畏惧的呢？"）

Confucius said, "If I examine myself and find no fault, what is there for me to fear?" (*The Analects*)

péngyǒu 朋友

Friends

志气相投而能相互补益的人。它是非亲族的人之间所建立的亲密的社会关系，属于儒家认为的"五伦"之一。"朋"本义是上古货币单位，象两串系在一起的贝（或玉），引申为"同门"，指一师之徒，即在一起相互切磋砥砺、探究学问和道义的人；"友"的古字形象方向相同的两只手，引申为"同志"，即志趣、志向相同的人。这种关系的建立和维系，对于超越血缘关系的社会构建及人格养成至关重要。为此，中国人历来崇尚以道义为其根本原则，而以诚信为其基本规范。人与人如此，国与国亦如此。

Pengyou (朋友) are people who are not kin but share the same aspirations and sentiments and can help each other. Representing a close social relationship between these people, friendship is one of the "five relationships" among humans defined by Confucianism, namely, relationships between father and son, sovereign and subject, husband and wife, elder brother and younger brother, and between friends. *Peng* (朋) originally was an ancient monetary unit resembling two bunches of shells or jade stringed together. It was extended to mean disciples who follow the same teacher, namely, people who study together to improve each other's knowledge and moral behavior. An ancient ideographic form of the character *you* (友) was two hands reaching in the same direction, which means comrades sharing the same interests and goals. The creation and fostering of this relationship is crucial to forming the society beyond blood ties, and to forming one's character as well. For this reason, the Chinese have always revered moral standards as their fundamental principle and integrity as the basic norm governing their relationships. This applies to both relationships between people and relations among countries.

引例 Citations:

◎君子以朋友讲习。(《周易·象下》)

(君子和朋友一道讲求学问、研习道义。)

A man of virtue joins his friends in pursuing learning and studying Dao. (*The Book of Changes*)

◎父子有亲，君臣有义，夫妇有别，长幼有序，朋友有信。(《孟子·滕文公上》)

(父子之间有骨肉之亲，君臣之间有公正之道，夫妻之间有内外之别，老少之间有尊卑之序，朋友之间有诚信之德。)

Between father and son, there should be affection; between sovereign and minister, righteousness; between husband and wife, attention to their separate roles; between old and young, a proper order; and between friends, honor and trust. (*Mencius*)

◎《礼记》曰："同门曰朋，同志曰友。"朋友之交，近则谤其言，远则不相讪。一人有善，其心好之；一人有恶，其心痛之。货则通而不计，共忧患而相救。(《白虎通义 · 三纲六纪》)

(《礼记》上说："共同研习的人称为'朋'，志趣相投的人称为'友'。"朋友相处，关系近的话，就相互问难毫不留情；关系远的话，就留一些情面。一人有善言善行，大家由衷感到喜爱；一人有恶言恶行，大家由衷感到痛惜。钱财通用而不斤斤计较，共同承担忧患而互相救助。)

It is said in *The Book of Rites*: "People who study together are called friends, so are those who share similar interests and aspirations. If friends are close, they ask each other tough questions. If they are not so close, they ask each other questions in a soft way. If one is decent in what he says or does, he will be loved. If one is ill-intentioned in what he says or does, he will be deplored. Friends share wealth without haggling over how it should be distributed, and they come to each other's aid in time of adversity. (*Debates of the White Tiger Hall*)

qīqíng-liùyù 七情六欲

Seven Emotions and Six Desires

七种情感与六种欲望。"七情"之说出自《礼记 · 礼运》，是指喜、怒、哀、惧、爱、恶、欲等七种人的情感。"六欲"之说最早见于《吕氏春秋 · 贵生》，指人欲生、恶死以及耳、目、口、鼻等器官对于声音、颜色、滋味、香味的欲求。后人将“七情”与“六欲”并举，泛指人的各种情感与欲望。“七情六欲”是人天生自然的本能，需要获得适当的抒发或满足，但同时也要有所节制。

This refers to various human emotions and desires. The term “seven emotions” comes from *The Book of Rites*, referring to happiness, anger, sadness, fear, love, hatred, and desire. The term “six desires” first appeared in *Master Lü's Spring and Autumn Annals*, referring to human desire for life, desire against death, and the desires of human organs such as ears, eyes, mouth and nose for sound, color, taste and aroma. Later, the term “seven emotions and six desires” came to be used to describe people's emotions and desires in general. Such emotions and desires, being naturally born with people, should be released or satisfied as appropriate. But they should not become excessive.

引例 Citations:

◎何谓人情？喜、怒、哀、惧、爱、恶、欲，七者弗学而能。（《礼记·礼运》）

（什么是人的情感？欢喜、愤怒、哀伤、恐惧、喜爱、厌恶、欲求，这七者是人不需要学习就会的。）

What are human emotions? They are happiness, anger, sadness, fear, love, hatred, and desire which are naturally born with people. (*The Book of Rites*)

◎所谓全生者，六欲皆得其宜也。（《吕氏春秋·贵生》）

（所谓保全生命，是指人的六种欲望都得到适当的安顿。）

Preserving life means satisfying people's justified desires. (*Master Lü's Spring and Autumn Annals*)

qìjié 气节

Moral Integrity

指人的志气和节操。志气即志向以及为实现志向而显示出的强大精神动力，如信念、勇气等；节操即对自身德行和合于道义行为的守护与坚持。今泛指坚持正义，在任何威逼利诱面前不屈服、不动摇的精神品质。这种精神品质为历代正义之士所崇尚，被认为是立身处世的根本所在。中华民族数千年，历经磨难而能长盛不衰、生生不息，与此密切相关。

This term means high aspiration and moral principles. Aspiration refers to the powerful innate drives such as beliefs and courage that underpin one's ambition and enables its realization, whereas moral principles guard and sustain one's moral and righteous behavior. Today, the term in a general sense means to uphold justice as well as an undaunted spirit that remains unwavering and unyielding before any coercion and seduction. This type of spiritual quality has been championed by men of justice throughout generations and is regarded as the bedrock to anchor oneself in the world. For several thousands of years, this principle of moral integrity has guided China through thick and thin towards prosperity and longevity.

引例 Citations:

◎ [汲黯] 好学，游侠，任气节。(《史记・汲郑列传》)

(汲黯好学，行侠仗义，注重志气节操。)

Ji An is keen on study, is gallant, and adhering to moral integrity. (*Records of the Historian*)

◎论人才当以气节为主。气节者，小有过当容之；邪佞者，甚有才当察之。（《宋史·陈俊卿传》）

（评论、选拔人才，应当以气节作为主要标准。有气节的人，即使有小的过错，也应当宽容他；而奸邪小人，即便很有才能，也应该仔细考察他。）

When considering and selecting talents, people should focus on an individual's moral integrity. A person with integrity can be selected in spite of his minor flaws, whereas a talented person with mean spirit should be closely scrutinized. (*The History of the Song Dynasty*)

◎功名富贵逐世转移，而气节千载一日。（洪应明《菜根谭》）

（功名和富贵随着时代的变迁而转移，但气节千百年长留人间。）

Fame and wealth come and go as times change, but moral integrity lives on forever. (Hong Yingming: *The Roots of Wisdom*)

qìwǎng-lìgǔ 气往轹古

A Piece of Writing with Appeal Surpasses That of Ancient Writers.

文章的气势、气概等超越古人。这里的“气”的含义很广泛，指文章的气势、气概，也兼指作品所蕴含的作家个人的精神气质、气节；“往”，过往，指“气”所经行之处；“轹”，本义是车轮碾过，引申为超越。这是南朝刘勰（465？—520？或532？）在《文心雕龙·辨骚》中对于屈原（前340？—前278？）作品的特点所作的概括，后成为文艺创作的一种自觉追求。

This term refers to a powerful appeal in writings surpassing that of ancient writers. Here *qi* (气) has a wide range of meanings, from an essay's powerful appeal to a writer's charisma or moral integrity. *Wang* (往) describes a channel through which such a vital force passes. *Li* (轹) literally means a wheel crushing something when rolling over it and metaphorically an overwhelming advantage over something. This is how Liu Xie (465?-520? or 532?) of the Southern Dynasties, in *The Literary Mind and the Carving of Dragons*, described the powerful appeal of Qu Yuan's (340?-278? BC) works. Writers of later generations invariably sought to create a powerful appeal in their writings.

引例 Citation:

◎固知《楚辞》者，体宪于三代，而风杂于战国……故能气往轹古，辞来切今，惊采绝艳，难与并能矣。（刘勰《文心雕龙·辨骚》）

（可以肯定，《楚辞》取法于三代的圣贤之书，但也掺杂有战国的风气……所以气概能超越古人，而辞藻又横绝后世。这种惊人的文采和绝美的华艳，是很难有作品比得上的。）

There is no doubt that *Odes of Chu* drew inspiration from ancient classics. But it also has some stylistic features of the Warring States Period... That is why it surpasses the works of ancient poets in terms of appeal and the works of later generations in terms of the rhetoric splendor. Such powerful appeal and splendor are unrivaled. (Liu Xie: *The Literary Mind and the Carving of Dragons*)

qīnrén-shànlín 亲仁善邻

To Be Benevolent and Friendly Towards Neighboring Countries

亲近仁德而与邻国友善。"仁"，狭义的理解指仁者即有仁德之人，广义的理解指仁德、仁义实即道德；"亲仁"表示的是对道德、正义的主动亲近与遵循；"邻"原指相邻的国家，亦可泛指近邻。这一思想最早见于《左传》，中国古人用它作为处理与相邻国家关系的重要指导原则，即邻国之间应当相互尊重、相互友好，共同构筑祥和安定的周边环境，它符合国家和民众的根本利益。从地缘政治角度看，"亲仁善邻"重视国与国之间的友好与和平，和"唇亡齿寒"有相通之处；但它又强调"亲仁"是建立"善邻"关系的基础和前提，即双方都应当共同遵循仁德。它体现了原则性和务实性相统一的国际关系理念以及中华民族崇尚"仁"与"协和万邦"的基本精神。

To be benevolent and friendly towards neighboring countries was first mentioned in *Zuo's Commentary on the Spring and Autumn Annals*. The ancient Chinese used this notion as an important guiding principle in handling relations with neighboring countries: Countries should respect and be friendly to each other, and jointly foster a benign and stable environment. This is in the fundamental interests of all countries and their people. In terms of relations among countries, the pursuit of benevolence and good-neighborliness emphasizes friendship and peace between countries and is similar to the idea that if the lips are gone, the teeth will be cold. This concept also emphasizes moral values as a basis of good-neighborly relations, that is to say, both sides should be guided by moral values in handling their relations. The concept, as applied to international relations, is one of both principle and pragmatism.

It embodies the Chinese nation's pursuit of harmonious relations with other nations based on moral values.

引例 Citations:

◎亲仁善邻，国之宝也。(《左传·隐公六年》)

（亲近仁德而与邻国友善，这是国家的法宝。）

To be benevolent and friendly towards neighboring countries is fundamental policy a country should pursue. (*Zuo's Commentary on The Spring and Autumn Annals*)

◎夫亲仁善邻，古之令轨。(《魏书·许谦传》)

（亲近仁德而与邻国友善，这自古就是国家的良法。）

To be benevolent and friendly towards neighboring countries – this has been a good principle observed by our country since its early days. (*The History of Northern Wei*)

◎亲仁善邻，国之美事。其或犹豫以至用兵，夫谁所乐为也？（《元史·外夷传一·日本》）

（亲近仁德而与邻国友善，这对国家来说是好事。或许有时会有迟疑偏离，甚至于发生战争，可又有谁乐意这样做呢？）

To be benevolent and friendly towards its neighbors is obviously in the interest of a country. It is true that sometimes a country may deviate from this policy, and this may even lead to war. But surely no one wants this to happen. (*The History of the Yuan Dynasty*)

qún 群

Group

群体或聚集成群。“群”指人在一定范围内聚集在一起。聚集成群是人的基本生存状态。聚集的人群会在人与人之间、人与群体之间形成某种关系或秩序。有序的群体能够为个体的生存提供必要保障。同时，良好而稳定的群体秩序也是群体不断繁衍发展的重要条件。

Qun (群) means a group or to form a group. A *qun* consists of people gathered together within defined limits. The formation of groups is a fundamental state of human existence. Among human groups, various relations and hierarchies will form between individuals and between individuals and the group. An orderly group can provide the security necessary for survival of individuals. At the same time, good and stable group order is an important condition for the continuous flourishing and development of the group.

引例 Citations：

◎子曰：“君子矜而不争，群而不党。”（《论语·卫灵公》）

（孔子说：“君子端庄而不争竞，聚集成群而不结成私党。”）

Confucius said, “A man of virtue acts with decorum and does not compete; he joins groups but does not form factions.” (*The Analects*)

◎水火有气而无生，草木有生而无知，禽兽有知而无义，人有气、有生、有知，亦且有义，故最为天下贵也。力不若牛，走不若马，而牛马为用，何也？曰：人能群，彼不能群也。人何以能群？曰：分（fèn）。分何以能行？曰：义。（《荀子·王制》）

（水火由气构成但没有生命，草木有生命而没有知觉，禽兽有知觉而没有道义，人有气、有生命、有知觉，而且还有道义，因此是天下最高贵的。人的力量不如牛，奔跑的能力不如马，但牛马却被人驱使，是什么原因呢？回答道：因为人能够组成分工协作的群体，那些牛马不能。人依据什么能够组成分工协作的群体？回答道：依靠名分差等。名分差等依据什么能够施行？回答道：依据道义。）

Fire and water have energy (*qi*) but no life. Grass and trees have life but are not sentient. Birds and beasts are sentient but do not understand what is right. Humans have energy, they have life, they are sentient and they also understand what is right, hence they are supreme. They are not as strong as oxen, nor as swift as horses, yet they can use oxen and horses – why is that? Because humans can form groups with a division of labor whereas oxen and horses cannot. Why can humans form such groups? Because they can differentiate their roles based on titles and ranks. Why can they differentiate their roles and ranks? Because they understand what is right. (*Xunzi*)

rénwénzhīyuán 人文之元

The Origin of Human Culture

意指人类文明文化的起源。元：起始，开端。这一术语的意义在于试图解释“人文”何以发生的原因。“人文”与“天文”“地文”是同级相对的概念。“天文”指天体、天气的运行变化及其规则，“地文”指山川河流等地貌及其走向。人居其中，因为有性灵、有思想，因而产生“人文”。“人文”指人类社会的礼乐教化、典章制度，尤指精神文明的创造活动及其产品，如文学、艺术、哲学等。考察人文起源，有助于阐明文学艺术等的基本性质，也可更好地把握其发展规律。只是，对于到底什么是“人文之元”，目前并无定论。南朝刘勰（465？—520？或 532？）的观点影响最大，他提出“人文之元，肇自太极”。但何谓“太极”，又成为学者聚讼的题目。因此，对于“人文之元”的解释，不妨宽泛一些，可理解为亘古之初先民生存于宇宙天地间时的思维情感活动，因其具有原始性质，与天地自然的关联十分密切，所以远古先民对于宇宙人生的认识较之今人更加本真。

This term aims to explain how human culture arose. It stands in contrast to what is known as "heaven's ways" or "earth's ways," the former referring to laws governing the movement and change of heavenly bodies and weather, while the latter to that of topographic features and directions of mountains and rivers. Since humans came into being with their spiritual pursuits and thoughts, human culture has thrived and prospered. Human culture, as encapsulated in this term, is taken to mean education in etiquette and music, laws and regulations, and especially outcomes of creative endeavor such as art, literature, and philosophy. A close inquiry into these origins can help to clarify the essential character of art and literature, and enable us to better grasp the laws of their development. However, dispute remains as to the precise meaning of the term. The most influential view was raised by Liu Xie (465?-520? or 532?) of the Southern Dynasties. He held that human culture had its origins in *taiji*, namely the supreme ultimate. But scholars continued to argue about the exact meaning of *taiji*. So the origin of human culture should perhaps be interpreted more broadly as the sum total of feelings and thoughts of our prehistoric ancestors who grappled with their existence between heaven and earth. Such feelings and thoughts were primitive and related closely to the natural world, so it can be safely said that those earliest inhabitants of the earth understood the universe and life in a more original way than people of today.

引例 Citations：

◎［刚柔交错，］天文也；文明以止，人文也。观乎天文，以察时变；观乎人文，以化成天下。(《周易·彖上》)

(［刚柔相互错杂，］是天的法则；礼仪昌明有所节制，是人伦的法则。观察日月星辰的运行状态，可以知道四季的变换；考察诗书礼乐的发展状况，可以用来教化天下百姓、实现文治昌明。)

It is a law of heaven that the hard and soft interweave; it is a rule of humans that they should observe the rites and conduct themselves with restraint. By observing the movement of the constellations, we can learn about the change of seasons; by observing development of human culture, we can enlighten the people and build a civilized society. (*The Book of Changes*)

◎夫有必始于无，故太极生两仪也。太极者，无称之称，不可得而名。(《周易·系辞上》韩康伯注)

(有一定从无开始，所以太极产生了阴阳两仪。"太极"是没有名称的名称，没有办法给它命名。)

Whatever is must have come from what is not. Thus the supreme ultimate morphs into two opposites: yin and yang. The supreme ultimate is only a makeshift name. In fact, there is no way to name it appropriately. (Han Kangbo: *Annotations on The Book of Changes*)

◎人文之元，肇自太极，幽赞神明，《易》象惟先。(刘勰《文心雕龙·原道》)

(人文的源头，产生于天地未分之前的混沌元气，深刻阐明这种神秘幽微的道理，以《周易》中的卦象最早。)

Human culture originated from a chaotic vitality, which had existed before heaven and earth became divided. Manifestation of a divination in *The Book of Changes* was the earliest elaboration on this mysterious and abstruse message. (Liu Xie: *The Literary Mind and the Carving of Dragons*)

róngrǔ 荣辱

Honor and Disgrace

荣誉与耻辱。“荣辱”是对个人或群体在社会生活中的表现所给予的评价与反馈。“荣辱”的评判以社会认可的价值标准为依据。言行符合标准，会享有荣誉；违背标准，则会遭受耻辱。此外，“荣辱”也指个人或群体对自身言行表现的道德感受，即感到光荣或耻辱。这种自我的道德感受源自对价值标准的认同。不过，不同学派所主张的价值标准会有所差别。

Honor and disgrace are evaluations of and feedback on the conduct of individuals or groups. People are judged on socially accepted values. One is honored if one complies with these values in both words and actions; and one is disgraced if one violates such values. Honor and disgrace also refer to how individuals or groups regard their own conduct morally in terms of honor or disgrace. These moral sentiments originate from people's identification with values. However, different schools of thought tend to espouse different values.

引例 Citations：

◎先义而后利者荣，先利而后义者辱。（《荀子·荣辱》）

（优先遵守义的原则而后才考虑利益的人，会享有荣誉；优先谋求利益而后才考虑道义的人，会遭受耻辱。）

Those who put righteousness before personal interests will be honored. Those who put personal interests before righteousness will be disgraced. (*Xunzi*)

◎知其荣，守其辱，为天下谷。为天下谷，常德乃足，复归于朴。(《老子·二十八章》)

（知晓荣誉，而接受羞辱，作为天下的低谷。成为天下的低谷，常德才能够充分发挥，回复到真朴的状态。）

One should value honor yet love disgrace, and accept the fact of falling deep into the valley. Being deep in the valley, however, means one can strive to cultivate virtue and return to the state of naturalness. (*Laozi*)

shàn shèng zhě bù zhēng 善胜者不争

Win a War Without Fighting

善于取胜的人不争斗。犹言“不战而胜”。战争的直接目的是战胜敌人，但战胜敌人并不以战争为最高手段，直接诉诸武力是不得已而采取的下策。面对冲突和争斗，应该在更高层次上寻求超越武力的更好的制胜方法。努力在各方面整备自身，使自身足够完备或强大，游刃有余，甚至没有对手，这是根本的制胜之道。

This concept means that the ideal way to win a war is not through fighting. The purpose of starting a war is to defeat the enemy; but defeating the enemy does not necessarily require a war, nor is war the ultimate means to triumph over the enemy. Direct use of force is the last resort, not the preferred option. In the face of conflict and rivalry, one should develop more effective ways of winning victory without using force. Strive to fully prepare oneself in every way, and make oneself strong enough to respond to all eventualities, to the extent that no opponent will emerge. This is the fundamental way to win victory.

引例 Citations：

◎天之道，不争而善胜，不言而善应，不召而自来，繟（chǎn）然而善谋。（《老子·七十三章》）

（自然的法则是，不争斗而善于取得胜利，不说话而善于得到回应，不召唤而使人自动归向自己，舒缓从容而善于谋划。）

The laws of nature are: to win a war without fighting; to have response without speaking; to solicit support without issuing a call; and to plan with ease. (*Laozi*)

◎善用兵者，先自修理不可胜之道。（《太平御览·兵部五十三·胜》）

（善于打仗的人，先整治确保自己立于不败之地的方法。）

One skilled at warfare first develops a way to make himself invincible. (*Imperial Reader for Emperor Taizong of the Song Dynasty*)

◎善胜者不争，善阵者不战。（张拟《棋经·合战篇》）

（善于取胜的人不争斗，善于布局的人不开战。）

One who is good at winning does not need to fight, and one who is good at making advanced plan does not need to start war. (Zhang Ni: On the Playing of Go)

shàn zhàn zhě qiú zhī yú shì 善战者求之于势

A Person Skilled at Warfare Seeks Victory Through Strategic Positioning.

善于打仗的人会凭借或造成对自己有利的态势以取得胜利。"势"即态势，指敌我双方军事力量的部署和行动所形成的整体局面或状态。它蕴含着巨大势能，是影响作战胜败的关键因素。有利的态势不是现成的，而是要通过合理的力量配置或部署、采取灵活机动的战略战术等主体能动的努力，最大限度地发挥己方优势、削弱敌方优势造成的。而谋势、造势、用势，使之有利于己而不利于敌，则是军事指挥官的重要职责。这一思想，后来超越军事范畴，成为商、政等诸领域领导者的智慧。

A person skilled at warfare will achieve victory by using or creating a strategic position favorable to himself. A "strategic position" refers to the overall situation or state resulting from the deployment and actions of two opposing forces. A strategic position can be enormously powerful and is a critical factor which affects victory and defeat. A favorable strategic position is not ready-made; it is created by the logical allocation or deployment of forces, efforts to take the initiative in employing flexible strategies and tactics, maximizing one's own strengths and minimizing the opponent's strengths. Planning, creating, and using a strategic position that is advantageous for oneself and disadvantageous for the foe is an important responsibility of military commanders. This concept was later extended beyond the military sphere and became part of leadership wisdom for business and governmental affairs.

引例 Citations:

◎势者，因利而制权也。(《孙子・始计》)

（所谓势，就是根据对自己有利的原则而采取相应的举措。）

Creating a strategic position means using what favors you and taking appropriate measures to gain control. (*The Art of War*)

◎故善战者，求之于势，不责于人，故能择人而任势。任势者，其战人也，如转木石。……故善战人之势，如转圆石于千仞之山者，势也。（《孙子·兵势》）

（所以善于打仗的人会凭借或造成对自己有利的态势以取得胜利，而不是一味要求士兵死战，因而他能选择合适的人并顺应当前的态势。所谓顺应态势，就是他指挥打仗，就像转动大木、巨石一样自如。……所以善于打仗的人，他所造成的有利态势，就像是把圆石从千仞高山上滚下来一样［不可阻挡］，这就叫作“势”。）

Therefore someone skilled at warfare achieves victory by using or creating a favorable strategic position, not just by having his troops fight. Hence he can choose the right people and adjust to the situation at hand. Adjusting to the situation at hand means that he can direct a battle as deftly as if he were rolling logs and boulders downhill… Thus the favorable strategic position created by someone skilled at warfare is as powerful as boulders rolling down the highest mountain. This is "strategic position." (*The Art of War*)

shàn zhàn zhě zhì rén ér bù zhì yú rén 善战者致人而不致于人

A Person Skilled at Warfare Controls His Opponents and Is Not Controlled by Them.

善于打仗的人能够调动敌人而不被敌人所调动。其要义在于强调掌握战争的主动权。在战场上，军队指挥官能驾驭战争并使之向着自己所期望的态势变化，是取得战争胜利的先决条件。战争的主动权以一定的客观条件和主观指导为基础，并随着敌我双方力量的消长和指导思想的正确与否而随时发生变换。战争的敌我双方，都力争在交战时间、地点选择及力量对比等方面将主动权掌握在自己手中。争取主动权的方法主要是运用灵活机动的战略战术，破坏敌之有利状态，造成敌之弱点，瓦解敌之斗志，阻止敌之意图实现，等等。主动权思想不只是很高的军事智慧，对其他领域的工作乃至为人处世等也有启发意义。

A person who is skilled at warfare controls his opponents and is not controlled by them. The key point here is an emphasis on controlling the initiative in a battle. On the battlefield, a prerequisite for victory is the troop commander's ability to determine the course of battle and steer it in the desired direction. Initiative in a battle is based on various objective conditions and subjective commands, and it constantly changes along with the changing balance of the opposing forces and the correctness of command concepts. During a battle, both sides try to take the initiative by controlling the time and place of engagement and the balance of forces. The main way to gain the initiative is to use flexible strategies and tactics to disrupt a situation which favors the opponent, to create weaknesses in him, to break his fighting spirit, and to thwart his plans. The concept of controlling the initiative is not only a manifestation of great military wisdom; it also offers insights for other areas of work and even for everyday behavior.

引例 Citations：

◎凡先处战地而待敌者佚，后处战地而趋战者劳，故善战者致人而不致于人。能使敌人自至者，利之也；能使敌人不得至者，害之也。故敌佚能劳之，

饱能饥之，安能动之。(《孙子·虚实》)

(凡是先到达战场等待敌方到来的一方是安逸轻松的，后到达战场仓促交战的一方则是疲劳的，所以善于打仗的人能够调动敌人而不被敌人所调动。或示以小利，诱使敌军自己进入我方指定的战场；或设法拦阻，使敌军无法到达相应的位置。所以，敌若安逸轻松，我则要设法使之疲劳；敌若粮草充足，我则要设法使之挨饿；敌若安稳驻扎，我则要设法使之移动。)

Whoever is first on the battlefield and awaits the foe will be rested, and whoever arrives late and rushes into battle will be tired. Hence one who is skilled at war can control his opponents instead of being controlled by them. He may use some small advantage to lure the enemy to a battlefield of his own choosing; or he may put the enemy at a disadvantage by preventing him from reaching the battlefield. Thus a rested enemy can be made exhausted, a well-fed enemy can be made hungry, and a settled enemy can be made to move. (*The Art of War*)

◎敌好击虚，吾以虚形之；敌好背实，吾以实形之。然而所击者非其虚，所背者非其实。故逸能劳之，饱能饥之，此所谓致人而不致于人也。(《宋史·兵志九·训练之制》)

(敌军如果想要攻击我兵力薄弱的地方，我即伪装成兵力薄弱的样子；敌军如果想要避开我兵力厚实的地方，我即伪装成兵力厚实的样子。但实际上，敌军所攻击的并非是我薄弱的地方，所避开的也并非是我厚实的地方。所以，敌军若安逸从容，我就要设法使之疲劳；敌军若粮草充足，我就要设法使之挨饿。这就是所谓调动敌人而不被敌人所调动。)

If the enemy wants to attack me where I am weak, I make my forces pretend to be weak; if he tries to avoid me where I am strong, I make my forces appear to be strong. But in fact the enemy will not be attacking me where I am weak, nor will he be avoiding me where I am strong. Thus if the enemy is relaxed I will try to exhaust him, and if he is well-fed I will try to make him go hungry. This is known as controlling one's opponent and not being controlled by him. (*The History of the Song Dynasty*)

◎多方以致敌之来，我据便地而待之，无有不胜。法曰："致人而不致于人。"（《百战奇略・致战》）

（千方百计调动敌人前来交战，我则占据有利地形以逸待劳，这样没有不打胜仗的。诚如兵法所说："调动敌人而不被敌人所调动。"）

I will use every means possible to entice the enemy into battle, where I await him at a place where the terrain is favorable to myself. This way I am assured of victory. As the book on warfare says, "Control others and do not be controlled by them." (*Extraordinary Strategies for Various Types of Battles*)

shèngwáng 圣王

Sage King

具有圣德的君王。具备圣德之人，即"圣人"，能够基于对天道、人心的把握，制定、规范人伦生活的秩序与法则，其所言所行成为人伦世界的至高典范。如果君王能够具备此种圣德，即被尊为"圣王"。在儒家的观念中，"圣人"居于王位是最理想的政治状态。但自孔子（前551—前479）以降，儒家所认可的"圣人"往往不得君王之位。

A king of great virtue, namely, a sage, by observing the way of heaven and based on his understanding of human nature, establishes social norms and laws to regulate public lives. What he says and does are thus the model for all to follow. If a king possesses such great virtue, he is called a sage king.

According to Confucianism, if a sage becomes the king, he would create an ideal state of governance. However, those whom Confucian scholars considered as sages never had the opportunity to become kings after Confucius' (551-479 BC) time.

引例 Citations:

◎辨莫大于分（fèn），分莫大于礼，礼莫大于圣王。（《荀子·非相》）

（分辨事物最重要的莫过于确定名分，确定名分最重要的莫过于制定礼仪，制定礼仪最重要的莫过于效法圣王。）

Determining social status is most important when it comes to distinguishing between things; establishing rites is most important for determining social status; and following sage kings is most important in establishing rites. (*Xunzi*)

◎故圣王修义之柄、礼之序，以治人情。（《礼记·礼运》）

（因此圣王确立义的根本原则、礼的秩序，用来治理人的情感活动。）

Therefore a sage king establishes the fundamental principles of justice and the order of rites to regulate human feelings. (*The Book of Rites*)

shí bì cháng bǎo, ránhòu qiú měi 食必常饱，然后求美

Attention to Refined Taste Comes Only After the Stomach Is Sated.

食物一定是先正常吃饱，然后再讲求口味。墨子（前468？—前376）主张节约和实用，反对文饰，认为过多的文饰既浪费劳动力，又浪费原材料。他提出先解决温饱，再满足审美。墨子并不是排斥美，也不是不会欣赏美，只不过他以实用性、功利性作为衡量美的标准，认为凡是不实用的、只

讲究形式华丽的都不是真正的美。儒家强调文质彬彬，将形式美与内容实质同等看待；而墨子则强调先质而后文。

Humans must first of all eat to live. Taste is secondary. Mozi (468?-376 BC) opposed extravagance in favor of frugality and utility. He argued that an extravagant way of life was wasteful of labor and raw materials. He prioritized eating one's fill and dressing warmly over aesthetic demands. It was not that he abhorred beauty or was unable to appreciate it. Rather, he adopted functionality and usefulness as his criteria for judging beauty, and believed that whatever was impractical or of only formal elegance had no true beauty. Whereas Confucian philosophers valued both form and content, arguing that external features and inner substance were equally important, Mozi placed substance well above form.

引例 Citations：

◎故食必常饱，然后求美；衣必常暖，然后求丽；居必常安，然后求乐。（刘向《说苑》引《墨子》）

（所以食物一定是先能正常吃饱，然后再讲求口味；衣服一定是先能正常穿得暖和，然后再讲求漂亮；居所一定是先能正常住着安稳，然后再讲求享乐。）

Hence, a person must be able to eat his fill before he can shift his focus to taste. He must dress warmly before he can consider elegance. He must also have a secure dwelling before he thinks about enjoying comfort. (*Mozi*, as cited in Liu Xiang: *Garden of Stories*)

◎古有无文者得之矣，夏禹是也。卑小宫室，损薄饮食，土阶三等，衣裳细布。当此之时，[黼]黻无所用，而务在于完坚。（刘向《说苑》引《墨子》）

（古代不讲究文饰的人明白这个道理，夏禹就是这样的人。他住的房屋又矮又小，他的饮食也是一减再减，土筑的台阶只有三级，他的衣服是用碎布缝制的。在夏禹那个年代，华美的样式基本派不上用场，人们追求的只是务必完好坚固。）

Sages of old times who shunned extravagance and pomp fully understood this. Emperor Yu of the Xia Dynasty was one such person. His cottage was both small and low, and he repeatedly cut expenditure on food and drink. There were only three earthen steps leading up to his cottage. His clothing was a patchwork of small pieces of cloth. In his days, excessive adornment was simply not helpful. People only required that things be durable and sturdy. (*Mozi*, as cited in Liu Xiang: *Garden of Stories*)

shì chū yú chénsī, yì guī hū hànzǎo 事出于沈思，义归乎翰藻

Recording History in an In-depth Way and Presenting It in Eloquent Writing

记述史实要深入构思，而归纳义理则要有华美的文辞。沈：同“沉”。出自梁昭明太子萧统（501—531）为其编纂的文学总集《文选》所作的序。它的意思是：史传体与编年体史书中的赞、论、序、述等文体，能通过深沉的构思，运用华美的语言，把历史事件、历史人物以及背后所蕴含的意蕴、规律表达出来。史传作品与一般文学作品不同，重在纪实并在文字中寓褒贬评价，但作为史传作品重要组成部分的赞、论、序、述，也具有一定的文学性，并形成独特的文体。后人往往用这一术语指文学作品的内容与特性。

This term stresses the need for both well-thought organization of content and its eloquent presentation in writing history. The character沈 (here pronounced *chen*) means "profound" or "in-depth." The term first appeared in the preface to *Selections of Refined Literature* compiled by Xiao Tong (501-531), Crown Prince Zhaoming of Liang during the Southern Dynasties. It means that sub-genres in historical biographies and chronicles, such as commendations, commentaries, introductory remarks and reviews, can, through in-depth organization of content and eloquent writing, better present historical figures and events and reveal things that shaped them. Unlike literary works, historical biographies are non-fictional and make either positive or negative comments on people and events. However, commendations, commentaries, introductory remarks and reviews, as important parts of historical biographies, also have literary value, thus creating a distinctive style. Scholars of later generations used this term to refer to particular types of content and features in literary works.

引例 Citation:

◎至于记事之史、系年之书，所以褒贬是非、纪别异同，方之篇翰，亦已不同。若其赞论之综缉辞采，序述之错比文华，事出于沈思，义归乎翰藻，故与夫篇什杂而集之。(萧统《文选序》)

(至于那些纪传体与编年体的史书，目的是为了褒贬是非、记载和分辨史实的异同，与崇尚文采的文学作品相比，已经有很大的不同。至于说到史书中的"赞""论"的综合编次要运用华美的词句，"序""述"文字的错综组织也须讲求文采，记述史实要深入构思，而归纳义理则要有华美的文辞，所以我将它们与诗文汇集编排在一起。)

As for historical biographies and chronicles, their purpose is to verify historical figures and events and make comments on them. So they differ from literary works, which prize eloquence in style. However, eloquent writing is also required for writing commendations and commentaries in historical books as well as introductory remarks and reviews. In a nutshell, history should be recorded in an in-depth way and presented in eloquent writing. I therefore place them together with literary writing in this book. (Xiao Tong: A Preface to *Selections of Refined Literature*)

shìyǔ-shànghuà 饰羽尚画

Inappropriate Embellishment of Writing

在色彩斑斓的羽毛上描画图案，比喻写作诗文时一味追求表面修饰和华丽辞藻。庄子（前 369？—前 286）以在彩色羽毛上描画图案为喻，认为孔子（前 551—前 479）过度推行教化，戕害了人的美好天性，破坏了人类社会素朴而美好的自然状态，结果适得其反。南朝刘勰（465？—520？或 532？）以此喻指文章和艺术作品过度追求形式美、违背自然美的不良风尚，承续孔子提出的“文质彬彬”的理念，明确了情理与辞采相统一的原则，由此形成以“中和”为美的古典美学思想。

This term describes the act of painting on a multicolored feather. Metaphorically, it means a love of ostentatious adornment in writing. Zhuangzi (369?-286 BC), by referring to the imaginary act of putting a pictorial pattern on a colored feather, contended that Confucius (551-479 BC) placed too much emphasis on education, thus killing the natural goodness of human beings and impairing the simple yet beautiful state of human society, confounding his original aspiration. Liu Xie (465?-520? or 532?) of the Southern Dynasties used this same example to hint at the harmful convention of excessively pursuing formal beauty in writing and other art forms at the price of natural beauty. He adopted the Confucian position of "matching form with substance," and set forth the principle of unity between rhetoric and meaning, thus forming the classic aesthetic of "balanced harmony."

引例 Citations：

◎仲尼方且饰羽而画，从事华辞，以支为旨，忍性以视民，而不知不信。（《庄子·列御寇》）

（孔子正打算过度雕琢文饰，致力于华丽的文辞，把枝节当主旨，矫饰自然性情以夸示于民众，不知道如此做法反而不会取得诚信。）

Confucius overestimates the value of adornment in writing and makes much of flowery wording. He mistakes insignificant details for the main message and shows off his skill at adding art to a natural flow of writing, not knowing that all this would lead to the opposite instead of winning trust. (*Zhuangzi*)

◎辞人爱奇，言贵浮诡，饰羽尚画，文绣鞶（pán）帨（shuì），离本弥甚，将遂讹滥。（刘勰《文心雕龙·序志》）

（文人们一味追逐新奇，文辞以浮华怪诞为贵，就像在色彩斑斓的羽毛上描画图案，在有装饰的衣带和佩巾上刺绣，偏离文章的根本已经很远了，几乎到了谬误泛滥的地步。）

The literati love to pursue novelty; they are obsessed with pomposity and grotesqueness. But this deviates so far from the essence of writing as to be appallingly erroneous, like painting a pictorial pattern on a multihued feather or performing embroidery on an already decorated waist strap or hand towel. (Liu Xie: *The Literary Mind and the Carving of Dragons*)

shūwén-zàishí 舒文载实

Use Fine Wording to Voice Feelings and Aspirations

诗歌的意义在于抒写文辞、传达情志。“舒文载实”属于诗歌创作论。“舒文”指组织安排词句，“载实”指承载、传达作者的情感心志，二者不可偏废。这一术语所传达的意旨，实际是儒家的文质观，即诗文创作要达到“文质彬彬”的均衡状态。如果只注重“文”，过多地修饰词句，文章就会显得虚浮；如果只注重“实”，又过于质朴粗野，文章则缺乏美感。故“文”“实”配合良好才是创作的首要原则。

The essence of poetry is to convey feelings and aspirations through fine wording. Fine wording involves the proper arrangement of words and sentences, while the voicing of feelings and aspirations constitutes the material content of poetry. Neither of these aspects should be neglected in favor of the other. The term taken as a whole reflects the Confucian view on the relationship between form and substance; that is, writing should achieve a balance between these twin demands. If the writer pays too much attention to form, his writing will sound supercilious. If he is over mindful of substance, it will sound crude and devoid of artistic merit. Therefore, a good combination of form and substance should be the primary principle of poetic creation.

引例 Citations:

◎是以“在心为志，发言为诗”，舒文载实，其在兹乎？（刘勰《文心雕龙·明诗》）

（因此，“藏在心里就是情感意志，用语言把它表达出来就是诗歌”，诗歌抒写文辞，传达情志，它的意义就在于此吧？）

Therefore, "if hidden in his heart, it is his feelings or aspirations. Once expressed in words, it becomes poetry." That is what the writing of poetry is all about, is it not? (Liu Xie: *The Literary Mind and the Carving of Dragons*)

◎故情者文之经，辞者理之纬。经正而后纬成，理定而后辞畅：此立文之本源也。（刘勰《文心雕龙·情采》）

（情感思想犹如文章的经线，文辞犹如文章的纬线。经线正了，纬线才能织成；情理与内容确定了，词句才能畅达：这是写文章的根本原则。）

Feelings and thoughts are akin to the vertical warp lines of a piece of writing, and wording akin to the horizontal weft lines. Only if warp lines are straight can weft lines be properly weaved together. Likewise, only if content and theme have been decided can wording become fluent. This is a fundamental principle of writing. (Liu Xie: *The Literary Mind and the Carving of Dragons*)

shūyě 疏野

Unrestrained and Ingenuous Spirit

洒脱不羁，真率自然。是唐代司空图（837—908）提出的二十四种诗歌风格之一，也是非常重要的古典美学范畴。“疏野”所反映的实际是诗歌创作中的一种“无心”状态，即任由本心本性与外物遇合，不从主观情志出发，不刻意选择外在景观与素材，不刻意运用某种手法、技巧，不精雕细刻、反复推敲。为文如为人，洒脱不羁，率真豁达，质朴自然。作为一种诗歌风格和创作心态，“疏野”并非任性、随意和没有章法，而是力求摆脱先入为主的观念甚至是潜意识影响，但是前理解结构、审美经验积累等依然会对创作起一定作用。它不仅代表一种自然天成、冲淡疏旷的美学风格，还表现了一种胸怀万物而又超然物外的生存状态与人生境界。

This term refers to one of the twenty-four styles of poetry as propounded by Sikong Tu (837-908) of the Tang Dynasty and falls into a very important classic aesthetic category. An unrestrained and ingenuous spirit reflects a state of "carelessness" in poetic creation, whereby the poet allows his inner self to encounter external things without constraint. It does not proceed from the poet's subjective feelings and aspirations nor does it choose any particular scenery and subject matter. It neither shows favor to any particular technique or means of expression, nor does it pay undue attention to wording. It encourages the poet to write just as freely, spontaneously, and naturally as he behaves in real life. As a poetic style and a creative mindset, an unrestrained and ingenuous spirit does not mean arbitrariness, petulance or lack of method. Instead, it aims to shake off the influence of any preconceived idea or subconscious thought, yet respect prior cognitive and aesthetic experience. It represents not only a natural, quietly elegant, and unrestrained aesthetic style, but also a magnanimous mind and an elevated state of being.

引例 Citations：

◎情性疏野曰闲。（释皎然《诗式·辩体有一十九字》）

（诗歌表现诗人洒脱不羁、率真自然的性情称之为“闲”。）

When a poet demonstrates a free and ingenuous spirit, he writes in a relaxed style. (Shi Jiaoran: *The Theory of Poetry*)

◎惟性所宅，真取弗羁。控物自富，与率为期。筑室松下，脱帽看诗。但知旦暮，不辨何时。倘然适意，岂必有为。若其天放，如是得之。（司空图《二十四诗品·疏野》）

（诗歌安随、寄寓情性，应当放任真性不加约束。心能控驭万物而意象自然宏富，表现自然真率当可预期。在松树下建造茅屋，摘下帽子自在读诗。只知道日出日落，哪管它何时何世。但求心情舒畅，哪想非要有所作为。就像这样顺任天性，便能体会疏野的意趣。）

Poetry flows spontaneously and embodies true feelings; it should give free rein to the poet's true self. Provided that his soul remains in control of all things and the images created by him are natural and wide-ranging, the poet can be expected to write in a natural, flowing style. He may build a hut under a pine tree, remove his hat, and read at ease. All that catches his attention is sunrise alternating with sunset. He hardly bothers about which time he is in. He pursues a carefree way of life without any higher goal. So long as he follows the natural course, he will experience the delights of a free, uninhibited life. (Sikong Tu: Twenty-four Styles of Poetry)

téngshēng-fēishí 腾声飞实

Fame and Accomplishment Survive Through Writing.

美好的名声借助文章而显扬，伟大的功业通过文章而流传。“腾”“飞”，在这里都是传扬的意思；“声”指“德音”，是与德行相随的美好名声；“实”指成就，是循道而建的功业。南朝刘勰（465？—520？或 532？）立足于古人所说的“三不朽”（立德、立功、立言）的人生最高目标，既视“立言”（文学创作）为传扬功德的手段，又视“立言”本身为一种功德，将写作文章的目的与文章自身的意义提升到“三不朽”的高度而融为一个有机整体。

Good reputation is spread through writing, as is great accomplishment. Here, both *teng* (腾) and *fei* (飞) stand for "soar high" and "spread far." *Sheng* (声) alludes to "fame achieved through virtue," while *shi* (实) refers to "accomplishment, especially that made by pursuing the correct way." Liu Xie (465?-520? or 532?) of the Southern Dynasties championed the "three highest attainments in life" as advocated by ancient Chinese sages, namely setting moral examples, performing great deeds, and spreading noble ideas. He regarded spreading noble ideas, or literary writing, not only as a means of promoting virtue, but also a virtue in itself. Thus he elevated the act of writing to the height of virtue, on a par with the two other attainments in life.

引例 Citations:

◎岁月飘忽，性灵不居，腾声飞实，制作而已。（刘勰《文心雕龙·序志》）

（岁月飘忽而过，生命和智慧无法永存，要想让美名显扬、功德流传，只有借助文章罢了。）

As time passes by, no life or wisdom can be preserved forever. To spread good reputation afar and promote virtue and merit, writing is indispensable. (Liu Xie: *The Literary Mind and the Carving of Dragons*)

◎爰逮宋氏，颜谢腾声。（《宋书·谢灵运传论》）

（于是到了南朝刘宋时期，颜延之、谢灵运在文坛声名鹊起。）

By the Song period of the Southern Dynasties, Yan Yanzhi and Xie Lingyun rose to fame in the literary world. (*The History of Song of the Southern Dynasties*)

tiānxià-yījiā 天下一家

All Under Heaven Are of One Family.

天下人亲如一家。“天下”既指全国所有的人，也指全世界所有的人。真正的爱，是超越血缘家族、超越国界的，与“博爱”“四海之内皆兄弟”等相类；甚至是超越人类，普被万物的，与“仁民爱物”“民胞物与”等相类。它同样昭示了中国人兼济天下的博大胸怀和敦厚仁爱的人文精神。

All the people under heaven are as close as one family. “All under heaven” here refers to all the people both in a country and in the whole world. True love transcends blood ties and territorial boundary. This term is akin to such expressions as “universal love” and “all are brothers within the four seas.” True love also transcends humankind and extends to everything in the world, as expressed in such phrases as “one should be kind to people and love things” and “you should consider all people as your kin, and all things as your own kind.” The term demonstrates the Chinese vision of caring and compassion for all.

引例 Citations:

◎今二国和好，天下一家，安得复论彼此？（《北齐书·阳斐传》）

（现在两国和平友好，天下亲如一家，怎能再分彼此呢？）

Now that our two countries are at peace and all under heaven are as close as one family, how can we continue to treat each other as outsiders? (*The History of the Northern Qi Dynasty*)

◎无不爱，是谓敦厚以居仁。……古人天下一家，中国一人，非意之也，其

心量原自如此。（黄宗羲《明儒学案·江右王门学案八·给（jǐ）谏罗匡湖先生大纮（hóng）》）

（无所不爱，这就是宽宏厚道而内怀仁爱之心。……古人做到天下亲如一家，全国如同一人，这并非是后人的臆想，而是古人胸怀本就如此博大。）

To love everyone and everything means to be broad-minded, kind, and benevolent... People in ancient times treated all under heaven as of one family, so all countrymen were united as one. This is not something imagined by later generations, but a true reflection of the broad-mindedness of the ancient people. (Huang Zongxi: *Commentaries on Writings of Famous Scholars of the Ming Dynasty*)

tiānzhí 天职

The Work of Heaven

天的职能或天所赋予的职责。“天职”具有不同的含义：其一，指“天”的职能。如荀子（前313？一前238）即认为，“天”能生成化育万物。这是“天”固有的职能，非人力所能为，也不是人可以求取的。其二，指“天”所赋予人的职责。由于“天”所具有的至高权威，“天”所赋予人的职责具有不可抗拒的应然的意义。

This term means heaven’s work, or a responsibility assigned by heaven. “Heaven’s work” can have different meanings. First, it can mean work done by heaven. For example, Xunzi (313?-238 BC) felt that heaven could give rise to all things. This is an inherent function of heaven; it is neither something humans are capable of, nor is it something they should seek to do. Second, it can mean a responsibility assigned by heaven to humans. Because the authority of heaven is supreme, a responsibility which it assigns is unshirkable.

引例 Citations：

◎不为而成，不求而得，夫是之谓天职。(《荀子・天论》)

（不去作为而成就了，不去求取而获得了，这就是所谓的天的职能。）

Achieving without acting, obtaining without seeking – this is called the work of heaven. (*Xunzi*)

◎弗与共天位也，弗与治天职也，弗与食天禄也。(《孟子・万章下》)

（不同他共享天赋予的职位，不同他一起完成天赋予的职责，不同他一起享有天赋予的福禄。）

He would not be shared the position given by heaven. Nor would he be shared the responsibility given by heaven, or the good fortune given by heaven. (*Mencius*)

tiānzhì 天志

The Will of Heaven

天的意志。出自《墨子》。墨子（前468？一前376）认为，“天”是最高的主宰，“天”的意志要求人们无差等地相互关爱，即“兼爱”。对于符合“天志”的人，“天”会给予奖赏；对于违背“天志”之人，“天”会施加惩罚。在“天”的不可抗拒的至高权威下，“天志”的好恶构成了人的言行以及人与人关系的根本准则。

The term comes from the book *Mozi*. Mozi (468?-376 BC) felt that heaven was the highest authority, and that heaven's will was for people to love one another regardless of rank, namely "universal love." Heaven would reward those who acted in accordance with its will, and punish those who contravened it. Given the supreme and irresistible authority of heaven, what it affirmed or rejected constituted the basic guidelines for people's words and deeds and for interpersonal relations.

引例 Citation:

◎天之志者，义之经也。(《墨子·天志下》)

（天的意志，是人奉行道义的准则。）

The will of heaven is the standard of what is right. (*Mozi*)

tǒnglèi 统类

Universal Principles

统括分别之物的法则。这一术语出自《荀子》。荀子（前313？—前238）认为，通过对事物的分类区别以及对不同类别事物的把握，圣人可以获得统括天下事物的普遍法则。"统类"保证了不同类别的事物在统一的秩序之中获得安顿与规范，同时也可以将新出现的事物纳入既有的秩序中来。

First proposed in the book *Xunzi*, this term refers to fundamental principles which apply to different things. It means that by differentiating things according to their categories and by understanding these categories, a sage could acquire universal principles which apply to all things. By following universal principles, one can ensure that different categories of things can all find their proper places within a unified order. At the same time, new things can also be integrated into the existing order.

引例 Citations：

◎倚物怪变，所未尝闻也，所未尝见也，卒（cù）然起一方，则举统类而应之。（《荀子·儒效》）

（怪异事物和诡异变化，如果从来没有听说过，从来没有见到过，突然于某处出现，那么可以通过统括事物类别的法则来应对。）

If strange things and developments which have never been heard of and never been seen before suddenly appear, they can be dealt with by applying universal principles. (*Xunzi*)

◎多言则文而类，终日议其所以，言之千举万变，其统类一也：是圣人之知也。（《荀子·性恶》）

（言论虽多但有文采而且条理分类清晰，整日议论的都是其立论的依据，他的言语虽千变万化，但其统括事物类别的法则是唯一的：这就是圣人的认知。）

His statements are many but they are always graceful and proper, and his classification is clear. Everyday, he expounded on his views. Though he expressed his beliefs in many ways, he is always guided by universal principles that apply to all things: this is how a sage observes the world. (*Xunzi*)

wángdào wú jìn gōng 王道无近功

The Righteous Way Seeks No Immediate Gains.

本指以仁义治理天下，不贪图眼前功利；后泛指遵循“正道”（正确的原则或方法），不急功近利。因为急功近利只能小成，不可能大成；而小成只能是暂时的，不可能持续长久，还可能偏离“正道”，带来无可挽回的后果，最终导致一事无成。胸怀大志，谋大事者，必然从全局、根本着眼，从长远考虑问题，始终依“正道”行事，不为一时得失而改变志向。其要义在于，大功无速成，正道须持守。

The term originally meant that in exercising governance, a ruler should act with benevolence and righteousness and not be tempted to seek immediate gains. Later, it came to mean the need to follow the righteous way, namely, sound principles or approaches, instead of seeking immediate gains. Such gains are not only petty and transitory in nature and unsustainable, but may also cause irreversible adverse consequences. Those who aim high should therefore focus on the big picture and long-term overall interests. They should always follow the righteous way and never allow themselves to be distracted by petty gains. The underlying message of this term is that no great accomplishment can be made quickly and easily and the righteous way must be followed.

引例 Citations：

◎岂知王道本无近功，成书亦非岁月哉！（项穆《书法雅言·功序》）

（岂不知以仁义治理天下不会很快奏效，学成书法哪有不费时日的呢？）

One should know that the righteous way of exercising governance does not produce immediate results, just as good calligraphy cannot be learned without years of practice. (Xiang Mu: *Right Ways for Learning Calligraphy*)

◎为学作事，忌求近功。一求近功，则自画气阻，渊源莫极。……圣人无近功，故至诚无息。（黄宗羲《明儒学案·诸儒学案中六·庄裕徐养斋先生问》）

（治学与做事，切忌急功近利。一旦急功近利，就会画地为牢，裹足不前，达不到最高境界。……圣明的人不图眼前的功利，所以能做到极其真诚，永无止境。）

One should not be tempted to seek quick and easy gains in either study or other pursuits. If one seeks quick gains, he will be short-sighted and cannot see beyond horizon… Sages are never distracted by immediate gains. That is why they can pursue the ultimate goal ceaselessly and with conviction. (Huang Zongxi: *Commentaries on Writings of Famous Scholars of the Ming Dynasty*)

wáng zhě zhī jì xī ér《shī》wáng 王者之迹熄而《诗》亡

The Book of Songs Died with the Decline of the Kingly Way.

圣王之道消失之后，《诗经》也就跟着衰亡了。一说“圣王之迹”专指西周时期周天子派人搜集民间诗歌、了解世风民情的事迹。“诗”指《诗经》，或说即指民间创作的诗歌。见于《孟子·离娄下》。这一术语揭示了文学与社会的关系。孟子（前 372？—前 289）倡导“王道”，他所说的“王者之迹”，实际上是他个人理想中的圣君社会以及相应的礼乐制度。“王者之迹”的消失，就意味着礼乐昌明时代的终结，也就是说《诗经》所依托的社会制度、政治生态变化了，歌咏于是也衰亡了，不可能再产生《诗经》那样的同类作品。而寓褒贬含义的《春秋》则应时产生，以适应礼崩乐坏时的社会现实需要。因为社会现实的变迁，从《诗经》到《春秋》，内容与形式都发生了变化。孟子的这种看法，是后代诗史关系批评理论的源头。

One explanation for the kingly way (圣王之迹) contained here is that it refers to the meritorious deeds performed by the monarchs of the Western Zhou Dynasty, when they sent their men among ordinary people to collect folk poetry and learn about local customs. Here, *shi* (诗) refers to *The Book of Songs*, or simply the verses created by the common people, as described in *Mencius*. The term sheds light on how literature relates to society as a whole. Mencius (372?-289 BC) was an ardent proponent of the kingly way, by which he expressed his longing for a saintly society with its corresponding system of rites and music. As such an ideal waned, the era of thriving rites and music drew to a close. With a fundamental change in social institutions and political climate, *The Book of Songs* lost the appeal it had once enjoyed, and the chanting of poetry also went out of fashion. Works of poetry similar to *The Book of Songs* could emerge no more. In its place, *The Spring and Autumn Annals*, a historical work known for its use of subtle and guarded language in criticism, appeared. This suited the needs of the new social conditions characterized by chaos and disorder, and explains the marked difference between *The Book of Songs* and *The Spring and Autumn Annals* in both style and content. This view, held by Mencius, became the source of poetry-related-to-history criticism.

引例 Citations:

◎王者之迹熄而《诗》亡，《诗》亡然后《春秋》作。（《孟子·离娄下》）

（圣王之道消失之后，《诗经》也就跟着衰亡了；《诗经》衰亡后，寓褒贬含义的《春秋》就产生了。）

The Book of Songs lost its popularity as the kingly way declined. In its place emerged *The Spring and Autumn Annals,* full of subtleties and implications. (*Mencius*)

◎春秋之后，周道浸坏，聘问歌咏不行于列国，学《诗》之士，逸在布衣，而贤人失志之赋作矣。（《汉书·艺文志》）

（自春秋之后，周朝的王道制度渐被破坏，各国之间的遣使访问及咏唱诗歌的礼仪不再实行，修习《诗经》的人散落到了民间，而贤能之士因得不到重用而表达失意心情的赋就产生了。）

Since the Spring and Autumn Period, the kingly way and institutions of the Zhou Dynasty had fallen into decline. Kingdoms no longer exchanged visits or practiced poetry-swapping rituals. Those who formerly studied *The Book of Songs* dispersed among the common folk, and wise men fell out of favor; hence the emergence of narratives, in a writing style known as *fu*, which show their authors' frustration and disappointment. (*The History of the Han Dynasty*)

wàngshìzhīshì 忘适之适

Effortless Ease

忘却了是否舒适，才是完全彻底的舒适。庄子（前 369？—前 286）认为人不能安宁的根源在于心灵本身，而非取决于外物。如果内心充满杂念，有过多的分别、计较之心，那么即便客观条件令人舒适，心灵也难以感到舒适。只有清除分别之心与各种杂念，才可能获得真正的舒适与安宁，甚至可以对抗令人不适的外部环境。

Only effortless ease is complete and thorough ease. According to Zhuangzi (369?-286 BC), people fail to achieve peace because they lack inner strength, not because of external factors. If the mind is full of distracting thoughts, always drawing a clear-cut line between all things and weighing gains and losses, then the soul will be ill at ease even though external conditions may be comfortable. Only if all attempts at differentiation are abandoned and all distracting thoughts eliminated, can true ease and tranquility be achieved, and even unpleasant external circumstances be resisted.

引例 Citations：

◎忘足，屦（jù）之适也；忘要（yāo），带之适也；知忘是非，心之适也；不内变，不外从，事会之适也。始乎适而未尝不适者，忘适之适也。（《庄子·达生》）

（忘记了脚，什么样的鞋子都舒适；忘记了腰，什么样的腰带都舒适；知道忘却是非之争，内心就感到舒适；不改变内心的持守，不顺从外物的影响，任何境遇下都会感到舒适。本心舒适就会无时无处不感到舒适，这就是忘却舒适的舒适。）

If a person forgets his feet, he will feel comfortable in any shoes. If he forgets his waist, he will feel comfortable no matter what waist strap he wears. Knowing how to forget questions of right and wrong, he will feel relaxed and peaceful. He will feel so under any circumstances so long as he maintains his integrity and takes care not to fall under the influence of external matters. If he feels at ease in mind, he will feel so anytime, anywhere. This is effortless ease. (*Zhuangzi*)

◎身适忘四支，心适忘是非。既适又忘适，不知吾是谁。（白居易《隐几（yìnjī）》）

（身体舒适就忘记了四肢的存在，心灵舒适就忘记了是非的存在。既舒适又忘记舒适，乃至忘记了自己是谁。）

If a person feels physically well, he will forget the existence of his limbs. If he feels spiritually well, he will forget the existence of right and wrong. His effortless ease will be such that he is no longer aware of his own existence. (Bai Juyi: At My Desk)

wěi 伪

Human Modification; Artifice

人为的修饰。"伪"指人为，引申而有不同的含义：其一，是相对于天生自然而言，"伪"意味着后天通过人为的方式，对天生的属性或能力所做出的修饰和改变。这种修饰体现着人伦生活中道德、礼法对人的规范。荀子认为"伪"对于天性的修饰是必要的。其二，是相对于真实而言，"伪"意味着通过人为的修饰来遮蔽真实的样态，具有虚假、欺诈的意义。

Wei (伪) means artifice, or modification by humans. *Wei* originally meant "by people," and by extension it can have different meanings. First, in terms of nature, *wei* implies modifications and changes made by people to preexisting natural attributes or functions. Such modification exemplifies in daily human relations how humans are regulated by moral codes and rules of propriety. Xunzi felt that such modification of human nature was essential. Second, in terms of truth, *wei* implies the use of human behavior to mask the truth; this has connotations of falsehood and deception.

引例 Citations:

◎不可学、不可事而在人者谓之性，可学而能、可事而成之在人者谓之伪，是性、伪之分也。(《荀子·性恶》)

(不可以通过学习、勉力从事而为人所具备的，称之为"性"；可以通过学习、勉力从事而为人所具备的，称之为"伪"，这是"性"和"伪"的分别。)

Attributes that people have but cannot acquire through learning and working are called nature. Abilities learned or mastered through effort are called artifice.

Such is the difference between nature and artifice. (*Xunzi*)

◎智慧出，有大伪。(《老子・十八章》)

((为政)多用智慧，就会有严重的虚假欺诈。)

With great use of intelligence in governance comes great deceptiveness. (*Laozi*)

wèiyǔ-chóumóu 未雨绸缪

Get Prepared for a Rainy Day

趁着天没下雨，先把门窗或房屋修缮好。绸缪：缠绕，引申指修缮。比喻事先做好准备。它并不是为了防止意外发生，而是为了使可能发生的事情不会成为"意外"。它要求人们不要为眼前的情势所局限，而要对可能发生的变化或未来的情势有所预判，提前做好应对，也即所谓"深谋远虑""防患于未然"。它强调的是人的主观能动性或动态大局观。

The term literally means to get the doors, windows and even the whole house fixed before it rains. *Choumou* (绸缪) means "wrap and bind" with an extended meaning of "repair." The term is a metaphorical way of saying to get ready for any unexpected events beforehand. It does not mean to prevent accidents from happening, but to prepare for possible occurrences rather than reacting to something "unexpected." It requires that people should not be limited by what they see in the current situation, but be able to anticipate possible changes or future situations and get prepared ahead of time. It is similar to the concepts "think forward and deep" and "prepare for an accident before it happens." The term underscores proactive behavior on the part of people or the changing nature of an overall dynamic situation.

引例 Citation:

◎谋之不深，而行之不远。人取小，我取大；人视近，我视远。未雨绸缪，智者所为也。（张居正《权谋残卷·筹谋》）

（谋划不深，行动就不会长远。别人贪图小利，我则谋求大利；别人关注眼前，我则关注长远。未雨绸缪，这是真正有智慧的人所做的事情。）

One's actions will not have a far-reaching effect if they are not well thought out and planned. When others covet small profits, I seek big benefits; when others focus on what's close by, I devote my attention to what lies ahead. Get prepared for a rainy day is what wise people do. (Zhang Juzheng: *An Incomplete Book on Strategies and Tactics*)

wén bù miè zhì, bó bù nì xīn 文不灭质，博不溺心

Graceful Wording Should Not Conceal Content, and Intricate Rhetoric Should Not Drown Out the Author's Feelings and Thoughts.

华美的文饰不掩盖文章的内容实质，繁富的辞藻不淹没作者的思想情感。这一术语属于创作论，出自南朝刘勰（465？—520？或 532？）《文心雕龙·情采》。针对魏晋以来有的文人为了写作而造作情理，不得不依靠各种文饰来掩饰内容的空虚，刘勰初步讨论了文章形式与内容的关系问题。他继承《论语》“文质彬彬”的观点，强调文与质应当并重，形式与内容均衡相称，绝不可以文害质。

This term comes from the traditional Chinese theory of literary creation. It first appeared in *The Literary Mind and the Carving of Dragons* by Liu Xie (465?-520? or 532?) of the Southern Dynasties. Rebutting the way some men of letters had since Wei and Jin times taken to faking emotions or arguments just for the sake of writing, and relying on all kinds of flowery language to disguise the emptiness of content, Liu discussed in brief the relation between form and content. Assuming the idea of mingling graceful wording with substance propounded in *The Analects*, he advocated giving equal value to content and form. His belief was that a balance should be struck between these two, and meaning should not be sacrificed in the pursuit of beauty in form.

引例 Citations：

◎子曰："质胜文则野，文胜质则史。文质彬彬，然后君子。"（《论语·雍也》）

（孔子说："实质多于文饰则会言行粗野，文饰多于实质则会虚饰浮华。形式与实质配合适当，然后能成就君子的品格。"）

Confucius said, "When one's inner disposition is in excess of his outward grace, he will look uncultured; when one's outward grace is in excess of his inner disposition he will seem to be superficial. Only when his inner disposition and outward grace are in balance can he be a man of virtue." (*The Analects*)

◎夫能设模［谟］以位理，拟地以置心，心定而后结音，理正而后摛（chī）藻，使文不灭质，博不溺心，正采耀乎朱蓝，间色屏于红紫，乃可谓雕琢其章，彬彬君子矣。（刘勰《文心雕龙·情采》）

（要能够先设立一个格局来安排文章要阐发的内容，拟定一个基调来安顿文章要抒发的思想情感。思想情感安顿好了再配合韵律，内容端正了再铺陈辞采，这样就可以使华美的文饰不掩盖文章的内容实质，繁富的辞藻不淹没作者的思想情感。要使朱、蓝这样的正色光彩闪耀，红、紫之类的间色一概摒弃不用。这样才是修饰文章、使文与质兼备得当的君子行为。）

When writing an article, design a structure for discussing your intended content, and set a keynote for expressing your feelings and thoughts. Then support such feelings and thoughts with a metrical pattern and adorn such content with formal beauty, making sure that wording does not conceal content and intricate rhetoric does not drown out the author's feelings and thoughts. Make perfectly regular colors such as vermilion and blueness shine. Do not use in-between colors such as orange and purple. This, I insist, is what a proper man should do – adorning his writing by making it both beautiful in style and rich in content. (Liu Xie: *The Literary Mind and the Carving of Dragons*)

wúdài 无待

Depend on Nothing

无所依赖。出自《庄子·逍遥游》。庄子（前 369？ —前 286）认为，人和事物的存在无法脱离其所处的境遇，因而总会受到各种外在条件的限制和制约，即有所“待”。但人的心灵能够超越其所处的现实境遇，不为外物所束缚、牵累，从而达到一种自由、无碍的境界。这即是心的“无待”状态。

The concept first appears in *Zhuangzi*. According to Zhuangzi (369?–286 BC), people and things cannot exist independently of their context, and thus are always limited and constrained by various external conditions, that is, they depend on something. But since the human mind is able to transcend the reality of its context and is not bound by external things, it can thus achieve a free and unhindered state. This is the state of the mind having nothing to depend on.

引例 Citations:

◎若夫（fú）乘天地之正，而御六气之辩，以游无穷者，彼且恶（wū）乎待哉！（《庄子·逍遥游》）

（如果能顺应天地的法则，驾驭阴阳风雨晦明六气的变化，而悠游于无穷的境域，他还有什么需要依赖的呢！）

One will need to rely on nothing if he is able to follow the rules of nature, manage the changes of weather, and enjoy everything freely in the infinite universe. (*Zhuangzi*)

◎自此以下至于列子，历举年知之大小，各信其一方，未有足以相倾者也。然后统以无待之人，遗彼忘我，冥此群异，异方同得而我无功名。（郭象《庄子注》卷一）

（自此以下至于谈到列子之处，依次列举年岁与见识大小不同的角色，他们各自信从自己的认识，不足以相互胜过对方。然后统帅以无待之人，遗忘彼我的分别，暗中统合众多的差异，差异的各方都有所得而我不显露功名。）

From this point up until Liezi, people of different ages and insights are listed in turn. Each person clings to his own understanding and fails to convince others. Then if the thought of "a person dependent on nothing" is applied to the situation, the boundary between self and others will be forgetten, and the differences will be surreptitiously unified. Thus all the others gain while the self claims no merit. (Guo Xiang: *Annotations on Zhuangzi*)

wúyù 无欲

Having No Excessive Desire

没有过度的欲望。“欲”主要指人为外物所感而产生的欲求。这样的欲求作为人得以生存的必要条件，应该获得适当的满足。但过度的欲望会造成对自身生命的伤害，也会导致道德的沦丧及社会秩序的混乱。因此儒家和道家都主张“无欲”。此外，在道家思想中，“无欲”有时特指道对待万物、为政者对待百姓的一种态度，即为政者节制自身的欲望，不去刺激百姓的欲望。

Yu (欲) means desire people have when they are attracted by external objects. Such desire, as the condition necessary for existence, should be suitably met. However, excessive desire is detrimental to one's life and will lead to a decline in public moral and result in social chaos. So both Confucianism and Daoism are against excessive desire. In addition, in Daoist thinking, "having no excessive desire" refers to Dao's attitude towards everything and how those in power should handle their relations with the common people. Daoism believes that those in power should suppress their desire and refrain from arousing people's desire.

引例 Citations:

◎子曰："吾未见刚者。"或对曰："申枨（chéng）。"子曰："枨也欲，焉得刚？"（《论语·公冶长》）

（孔子说："我没见过刚正的人。"有人回应说："申枨就是。"孔子说："申枨欲望太多，哪里能够刚正呢？"）

Confucius said, "I have never seen any person of rectitude." Someone responded, "Shen Cheng is such a person." Confucius said, "Shen Cheng has too many desires. How can he be of rectitude?" (*The Analects*)

◎故圣人云：我无为而民自化，我好静而民自正，我无事而民自富，我无欲而民自朴。(《老子·五十七章》)

（所以圣人说：我无为则民众自己化育，我好静则民众自己端正，我不多事则民众自己富足，我不多欲则民众自然朴实。）

Therefore the sage said: "People know how to cultivate themselves when I do nothing to interfere. They will behave themselves when I keep quiet. They will prosper when I am out of the way; and they will be sincere and honest when I hold my desire in check." (*Laozi*)

xiàxué-shàngdá 下学上达

Study Concrete Things and Reach to a Higher-level Understanding

学习常见、具体的人情事理，进而掌握高深、普遍的道理。出自《论语·宪问》。本义指学人事，知天命，实际是倡导一种治学修身的精神，将自觉追求天命、天道作为毕生的使命和生命最高的境界。后来，"下"被阐释为"形而下"，即"器"，有形质的具体事物；"上"被阐释为"形而上"，即"道"，无形质的基本原理。其含义衍生为知其事，明其道；行其事，知其理。这种治学修身的思想，激励人不要满足于习得具体的事物或学会做具体的事情，还要进而达到对事物基本原理或普遍规律的认知，向着自身完满或高度自觉的境界而努力。其哲学基础是"道器无二""知行合一"。

The term means to study common and concrete human affairs and to progress from that to an understanding of higher and more universal truths. Coming from *The Analects*, it literally means to study human affairs and understand heaven's will, but is actually advocating a spirit of scholarship and self-cultivation which regards the pursuit of heaven's will and heaven's way to be the highest stage of one's life and lifelong mission. This is to mean that knowing something is to understand its truths, while acting upon something is to know its principles. This concept of scholarship and self-cultivation encourages people not to be satisfied with acquiring a specific object or learning a specific thing; rather, they should progress to acquiring knowledge of fundamental truths or universal rules, and strive for self-perfection or to reach a heightened state of self-awareness. The philosophical basis of this idea is that there is no distinction between Dao and objects, and that knowledge and action are one.

引例 Citations：

◎学在事时斯是理，盍于事上每深思？但令下学功夫到，上达之机便自知。（朱熹《训蒙绝句·下学上达》）

（弄通一件事即是知晓其道理，为何不在每件事上深思其道理呢？只要在基本的人情事理上所下的功夫到了，掌握至上道理的窍要也就自然领悟了。）

To comprehend something is to understand its principles, so why not always think deeply about the principles of everything? If only the study of common human affairs is thorough, one will naturally know how to grasp the highest truths. (Zhu Xi: *Sayings to Teach the Young*)

◎"形而上"与"形而下"不是两般道理，"下学""上达"不是两截工夫。（吕坤《呻吟语·内篇·谈道》）

（"形而上"和"形而下"不是两种不相干的道理，"下学"和"上达"也不是分作两段的功夫。）

"That which is below form" and "that which is above form" are not two unrelated truths; "studying concrete things" and "reaching to a higher-level understanding" are not two separate efforts. (Lü Kun: *Moan and Groan*)

◎先生之学，以“下学上达”为的，行之而后著，习矣而后察。真能行习，未有不著察者也。下学者，行也；上达者，知也。（黄宗羲《明儒学案·诸儒学案下三·给（jǐ）事郝楚望先生敬》）

（[郝楚望]先生的学问以“下学上达”作为根本宗旨，认为践行而后明白事理、熟习而后明辨是非。只要真能做到践行和熟习，没有不明白事理、分辨是非的。所谓下学就在于践行，所谓上达就在于获得真知。）

The key principle of Hao Chuwang's scholarship is "studying concrete things and reaching to a higher-level understanding." He argues that one understands principles after acting, and that one distinguishes right from wrong after becoming well versed in it. If one can truly act and become well versed in it, one can understand all principles and distinguish all right from wrong. So studying concrete things is to act, and reaching to a higher-level understanding is to acquire true knowledge. (Huang Zongxi: *Commentaries on Writings of Famous Scholars of the Ming Dynasty*)

xiánhuá-pèishí 衔华佩实

Harmony Between Substance and Style

既有华美的文辞，又有充实的内容。“衔”，含在口中；“佩”，佩戴在身上。“衔”“佩”在这里都是“具有”的意思。“华”，本指植物的花，喻指文辞、形式华美；“实”，本指植物果实，喻指文章内容充实。既有充实内容，又有华美形式，是一切文艺作品的理想形态，也是古今公认的写作诗文的基本原则。具体的诗文作品会存在偏重形式美和偏重内容充实的区别，具体到某一个作者也会有不同的审美偏好，但总体上须要保持均衡折中的状态。南朝刘勰（465？—520？或 532？）依据圣人经典确立了这一原则，既反对形式主义，也肯定了文采和形式技巧的重要性。

A literary work should be beautiful in wording and solid in content. *Xian* (衔) means "hold in one's mouth," and *pei* (佩), "put on." *Hua* (华) originally meant a "flower" and figuratively stood for "elegant language" or "formal beauty." *Shi* (实) originally meant "fruit" and figuratively signified "fullness of content." It has been widely accepted over the centuries that an ideal work of art gives equal weight to content and form. This is an essential principle governing the writing of prose and poetry since ancient times. Some works prioritize formal beauty and others focus on fullness of content. Likewise, different writers have different aesthetic tastes. But overall, a balance should be struck between these two merits. Liu Xie (465?-520? or 532?) of the Southern Dynasties established this principle on the basis of the works of the sages. While opposing formalism, he nevertheless recognized the value of formal beauty and technique.

引例 Citations：

◎然则圣文之雅丽，固衔华而佩实者也。（刘勰《文心雕龙·征圣》）

（既然如此，那么圣人的文章既雅正又华丽，本就兼有华美的文采和充实的内容。）

Thus the writings of the sages have class and beauty; they are graceful in wording and solid in content. (Liu Xie: *The Literary Mind and the Carving of Dragons*)

◎贻上之诗，文繁理富，衔华佩实。（钱谦益《王贻上诗集序》）

（王士禛的诗，文采繁富而意义丰赡，既有华美的文辞，又有充实的内容。）

The poetry of Wang Shizhen is both stylistically intricate and rich in meaning. It features both beautiful wording and solid substance. (Qian Qianyi: Preface to Wang Shizhen's Poems)

xīn shēng ér yán lì 心生而言立

Words Flow Forth from the Heart.

人有了思想感情，才产生语言。这一术语的意义在于指出了人的思想感情是语言同时也是一切文学创作的前提，人有了充沛真实的思想情感，才能写出上好的诗文。它体现了古人对于创作主体精神世界的重视。它还强调，由“心”到“言”，并非刻意的安排，而应是自然而然的过程。

Speech and writing come from feelings and thoughts. This term suggests that feelings and thoughts are the sources of language and all literary creation as well. Only when imbued with true feelings and thoughts will writers be able to produce good prose and poetry. It reflects ancient Chinese people's emphasis on the inner world of writers as creative subjects. The term also makes it clear that the process whereby words come from the heart is natural rather than artificial.

引例 Citations：

◎为五行之秀，实天地之心，心生而言立，言立而文明，自然之道也。（刘勰《文心雕龙·原道》）

（人是天地万物中最杰出的种类，实际是天地的核心与灵魂。心灵活动产生语言，语言表达出来就形成文章，这是自然规律。）

Man stands out among all species and is the essence and soul of the world. In the natural course of events, the desire to express man's inner self leads to the emergence of language, which in turn gives rise to literary creation. (Liu Xie: *The Literary Mind and the Carving of Dragons*)

◎凡音之起，由人心生也。人心之动，物使之然也。（《礼记·乐记》）

（一切音乐都起源于人的内心。人的内心之所以产生活动，是受到外物感发的结果。）

All music originates in people's hearts. Feelings arise in people's hearts as a result of external impact. (*The Book of Rites*)

xíngshén 形神

Form and Spirit

形体和精神，肉身与灵魂。这是中华生命哲学的一对重要范畴。就人的生命而言，此二者是统一而不可分的。二者合即是人生，二者分即是人死。但就二者的关系而言，则大致有两种相对的观点：一种观点认为精神是生命的本质所在，而身体则只是生命的寄居之所；另一种观点认为身体是精神存在的物质基础，而精神则是身体显示功用的内在根据。此外，这对范畴也用于指建筑的形制与内涵、文艺作品的形式与内容、形貌与神韵等，大体属于美学范畴。

Form and spirit, or body and soul, are an important pair of concepts in Chinese philosophy on life. In terms of human life, these two concepts exist in unity and are inseparable. Their unity gives rise to life, while their separation leads to death. There are generally two opposing views about the relationship between the two concepts. One view holds that spirit is the essence of life, while body is only the form in which life exists. The other view is that body is the material basis for the existence of spirit, while spirit is the inner basis for the functioning of body. This pair of concepts also apply to the realm of aesthetics, referring to the form and appeal of architecture, or the form and content as well as the form and charm of literary works.

引例 Citations：

◎凡人所生者神也，所托者形也。神大用则竭，形大劳则敝，形神离则死。……由是观之，神者生之本也，形者生之具也。（《史记・太史公自序》）

（大凡人存在生命是因为有精神，生命依托是身体。精神过度使用就会枯竭，身体过度疲劳就会损害，身体与精神分离就会死亡。……由此看来，精神是生命的内在根本，身体是生命的外在形式。）

All human beings exist because they have spirit, and their life depends on their bodies. If the spirit is overused, it will be depleted; if the body is overworked, it will be damaged; if body is separated from spirit, it will cease to exist... Thus, spirit is the inner root of life, and body is the outer form of life. (*Records of the Historian*)

◎形须气而成，气须形而知，天下无独燃之火，世间安得有无体独知之精?（王充《论衡・论死》）

（人的形体需要有气才能成为人，而气需要寄托于形体才能有认知，天下不存在没有物而能自燃的火，世间怎么可能有不依托形体而有认知的精气？）

The human body needs energy to become a human being, and energy needs to be in the body in order to be perceived. No fire can burn on its own. How can there be a vital essence without it taking a form? (Wang Chong: *A Comparative Study of Different Schools of Learning*)

◎神即形也，形即神也，是以形存则神存，形谢则神灭也。……形者神之质，神者形之用。是则形称其质，神言其用。形之与神，不得相异也。（范缜《神灭论》）

（精神即是形体，形体即是精神。所以形体存在，精神就存在，形体没有了，精神也就消失了。……形体是精神得以存在的形式，精神是形体显现功用的根据。所以说形体是就其物质形式而言的，精神是就其内在功用而言的。形体和精神是不可分割的一个整体。）

Spirit is form, and vice-versa. Therefore, if form exists, spirit exists; if form is gone, so is spirit... Form is the way in which spirit exists, and spirit is the basis for form to function. Therefore, form is material, and spirit is its inner function. Form and spirit are an inseparable whole. (Fan Zhen: On the Extinction of Soul)

xūhuái-ruògǔ 虚怀若谷

An Open Mind as Broad as a Mountain Valley

心胸像山谷一样深广。形容为人谦虚豁达，善于听取他人各种意见。这被认为是取得大成就的人以及领导者应该具备的良好品质。具备这种品质的人，能够接受各种意见甚至是批评、反对的声音，这样可以及时改正自身缺点或修正决策失误，吸引更多的人归向自己，使自己获得更多支持。此与“厚德载物”“有容乃大”相通。

This phrase describes a breadth of mind that is broad and open as a deep and expansive mountain valley. Metaphorically, it refers to a person who is modest, generous, and tolerant, good at listening to other people's opinions and taking them into consideration, which is a desirable characteristic deemed typical in eminent people and leaders. People with such a quality can accommodate various opinions, including criticism and objections. In so doing, they can make timely correction of their mistakes or amend erroneous policies, thereby attracting more people to join and support them. This term is similar in meaning to other concepts such as "having ample virtue and carrying all things" and "a broad mind achieves greatness."

引例 Citations：

◎古之善为士者，微妙玄通，深不可识。……敦兮其若朴，旷兮其若谷。（《老子·十五章》）

（古时善于行道的人，精微玄妙，神奇通达，深不可测而难以理解……他敦厚质朴啊，就像未经雕琢的木头；他空旷广阔啊，就像幽静的山谷。）

In ancient times, a person who is good at practicing Dao was seen as exquisitely insightful, magically capable, profoundly knowledgeable, and beyond the understanding of ordinary people... He looks simple and natural as a piece of uncarved wood; he is open and broad as a tranquil valley. (*Laozi*)

◎虚怀待人，人亦思附。(《资治通鉴·唐纪·德宗兴元元年》)
（心胸开阔，待人谦虚，人们都愿意归附他。）

A broad-minded person who treats others with respect has no problem attracting people eager and willing to follow him. (*History as a Mirror*)

◎虚怀若谷，宜其造诣之进而弥上也。（袁枚《随园诗话补遗》卷四）
（他虚怀若谷，因而他的诗歌造诣越来越高是理所当然的。）

He has an open mind as broad as a valley, which explains why he becomes increasingly better in poetic accomplishments. (Yuan Mei: *Addendum to Suiyuan Remarks on Poetry*)

xuánjiě 县解

Freeing the Mind from Bias

解除倒悬的状态（县:“悬”的本字）。也作“悬解”。出自《庄子·养生主》。庄子（前 369？—前 286）认为，人们往往站在自我立场上去看待他者，因而按照自己的标准形成对他者、对世界的成见，让自己的心处于某种执着的情绪或状态之中。在庄子看来，这种执着于内心成见的状态，就好像心被捆缚倒悬起来。而破除内心的成见，解除心被倒悬的状态，即是所谓的“县解”。

Literally, this term means to reverse the state of one being hung upside down. It originated from *Zhuangzi*. The author Zhuangzi (369?-286 BC) found that people tend to look at other people or things from their own positions, and they thus develop biased views about others and the world. Their mind is consequently in a state of tension. To Zhuangzi, this state of mind of clinging to one's prejudice is like one being bound and hung upside down. So, breaking free from subjective bias is like freeing one from this state of tension.

引例 Citation：

◎适来，夫子时也；适去，夫子顺也。安时而处顺，哀乐不能入也，古者谓是帝之县解。(《庄子·养生主》)

（正该来时，老子应时而生；正该去时，老子顺时而死。安于时命而顺应变化，悲哀和欢乐就不能进入内心，古时候称这样做是天然的解除倒悬。）

When time called, Laozi was born; when time was due, he passed away. When one follows the law of nature, he will not be disturbed by grief or joy. This was known in ancient times as a natural way of freeing the mind from bias or distorted perception, like freeing one from a state of being hung upside down. (*Zhuangzi*)

yán 言

Language

言语。“言”是人们表达思想、意愿以及相互交流的基本载体。对于“言”是否能够准确、完整地表达想法，尚存在争论。人们会出于各种原因，有意或无意地用言语遮蔽或错误地表达想法。此外，“言”有时也特指为政者对百姓的教化方式。儒家重视“言传”的作用，而道家则主张“不言之教”。

Yan (言) means language, or words. Language is the basic vehicle through which people express thoughts and wishes, and with which they conduct exchanges. There are still debates regarding whether or not language can accurately and completely express thinking. For various reasons, language may be used by people – deliberately or not – to obfuscate or erroneously express ideas. Moreover, *yan* at times specifically referred to a means by which those in government instructed the populace. Confucians stressed the role of "conveying through words," while Daoists favored "wordless instruction."

引例 Citations:

◎子曰："君子欲讷于言而敏于行。"（《论语·里仁》）

（孔子说："君子希望言语谨慎迟缓而行动敏捷。"）

Confucius said, "A man of virtue tries to be cautious with words but quick in action." (*The Analects*)

◎是以圣人处无为之事，行不言之教。（《老子·二章》）

（因此圣人以无为的方式处理世事，以不言的方式教导百姓。）

Therefore, sages deal with world's affairs by way of non-action, teaching people without uttering a word. (*Laozi*)

yán yǔ zhì fǎn, wén qǐ zú zhēng 言与志反，文岂足征

Writing That Runs Counter to Its Author's Aspirations Is Worthless.

如果所写文章与自己内心的情志不一致，这样的文章有何价值呢？"言"指言辞、文章，"志"指作者的思想情感。出自南朝刘勰（465？—520？或532？）《文心雕龙·情采》。刘勰认为，在创作的时候，应当为情而造文、为志而发言，就像《诗经》的创作者们那样，心中有志向、有愁思、有欢欣，然后发为歌咏，形成诗篇，自然就是佳作。如果所写与所想所感的不

一样，或者内心苍白、无病呻吟，如此写出的作品就毫无意义。这一术语批评了好尚浮华、忽视真情实感的现象。

If a piece of writing contradicts its author's aspirations, why bother to write it at all? Here, *yan* (言) stands for either "speech" or "writing," and *zhi* (志) refers to an author's feelings and aspirations. The term originates from *The Literary Mind and the Carving of Dragons* by Liu Xie (465?-520? or 532?) of the Southern Dynasties. In Liu's view, a writer should write to express his feelings and aspirations in the same way the authors of *The Book of Songs* did, bursting into songs and verses to voice their aspirations, sorrows and joys. Only such writings can be truly good. If what they put down on paper does not accord with what they think or feel, or if they themselves are soulless and can only show an affected sentimentality, their writings will naturally prove meaningless. This term criticises writers who are pompous and flashy to the neglect of true feelings.

引例 Citation:

◎夫桃李不言而成蹊，有实存也；男子树兰而不芳，无其情也。夫以草木之微，依情待实；况乎文章，述志为本。言与志反，文岂足征？（刘勰《文心雕龙·情采》）

（桃树、李树虽然不会说话，树下却被踩出了小路，那是因为它结出了甘甜的果实；从前有位男子种植兰花，开出的花却没有香气，那是因为没有相应的情感投入。像草木这样的细微之物，还得依赖情感投入［它才绽放香气］或者有待结出果实［树下才会踩出小路］；何况写作文章，就应该以抒写情志作为根本。如果所写的言辞与内心的情志不一致，这种文章还有何价值呢？）

Trees bearing peaches and plums do not have to talk, yet the world, attracted by the sweet fruits they yield, beats a path to them. A man once planted an orchid but its flowers did not exude any fragrance. Why? Because he did not put his heart into his cultivation. Even trees and flowers rely on sincere care to bear fruit or to give off a sweet scent. So it is with the business of writing, which is essentially about voicing one's feelings and wishes. If what is written contradicts the author's aspirations, what's the point of writing at all? (Liu Xie: *The Literary Mind and the Carving of Dragons*)

yílún 彝伦

Yilun / Constant Relations

常道。出自《尚书·洪范》。古人认为，人伦生活遵循着某些恒常不变的法则。这种恒常的法则，称为“彝伦”。“彝伦”源自对天道的效法与遵从，体现着“天”的权威。“彝伦”规范着人伦生活，保障了人伦生活的有序运转。为政者尤其是天子的首要任务就是把握并遵循这些恒常的法则。

The term *yilun* (彝伦), which corresponds to constant relations, first appears in *The Book of History*. In Chinese antiquity, it was believed that the relations of human life followed certain constant laws or *yilun*, which were derived from the imitation of and compliance with the heavenly way, and thus reflected the authority of Heaven. *Yilun* regulated the relations of human life and guaranteed its order. The primary task of the rulers, especially the Son of Heaven, was to grasp and follow these constant laws.

引例 Citation：

◎箕子乃言曰：“我闻在昔，鲧（gǔn）堙（yīn）洪水，汩（gǔ）陈其五行。

帝乃震怒，不畀（bì）'洪范'九畴，彝伦攸斁（dù）。鲧则殛（jí）死，禹乃嗣兴，天乃锡（cì）禹'洪范'九畴，彝伦攸叙。"（《尚书·洪范》）

（箕子于是说："我以前曾听闻，鲧封堵洪水，乱用了五行。上天于是震怒，不再赐予鲧九种大法，恒常的治国法则因此败坏了。鲧被流放至死，禹于是继承父业而兴起，上天将九种大法赐给了禹，恒常的治国法则因此恢复了秩序。"）

Jizi thereupon said: "I once heard that Gun misused the five elements, i.e., wood, fire, earth, metal and water, in his efforts to control the floods. The Ruler of Heaven was furious and deprived him of all the Nine Great Rules. As a result, the constant laws of statecraft fell into ruin. Gun was exiled until his death. His son Yu took over his father's duties and became very successful in harnessing the floods. Heaven bestowed the Nine Great Rules on him. Consequently, the constant laws of statecraft were restored to order." (*The Book of History*)

yǐwén-wéixì 以文为戏

Playful Writing

将写文章看作游戏，指用戏谑诙谐的笔法写作文章。唐朝著名文学家韩愈（768—824）创作了《毛颖传》《送穷文》等作品，以戏谑的形式和笔法表达严肃的主题，由此产生中国古代文论的一个术语。它强调文学的游戏愉悦功能，用戏谑诙谐的笔法摹写严肃庄重的社会主题，或将物拟人，或虚构情境，借以讥讽世情、寄托个人愤懑。这与儒家传统的"文以明道""文以载道"等观点形成了鲜明对比，成为当时争论的焦点。裴度（765—839）、张籍（767？—830？）等人对此理论与创作倾向持否定批评态度，而柳宗元（773—819）则力排众议，专门撰文阐释“以文为戏”的思想价值和审美意义。实际上，“以文为戏”与传统的文道观并没有本质区别，而且相互补充，各有其理论价值。韩愈、柳宗元的理论开拓和创作实践丰富并拓展了古文的文体形式，确立了“以文为戏”的文学史地位，深刻影响了后世的杂文创作。

This term refers to a playful approach to the composition of prose. Famed Tang Dynasty writer Han Yu (768-824), for example, wrote his "Biography of Mao Ying" and "Bidding Farewell to Poverty," both dealing with serious themes, in a witty way. Playful writing thus became a style of classic Chinese prose. It stressed the entertaining, game-like function of literature and playfully explored serious themes. Thus, a writer often personified a non-human object or conjured up a situation to satirize human behavior and express personal feelings. This playful approach to writing became highly controversial, as it stood in contrast to the established Confucian notion that literature should be a vehicle of cultivating moral values. Some scholars like Pei Du (765-839) and Zhang Ji (767?-830?) opposed this style of writing, but Liu Zongyuan (773-819) wrote an essay in support of Han Yu, arguing that playful writing had intellectual value and aesthetic significance, and it was in fact not that different from the tradition of regarding literature as a vehicle of cultivating moral values. These two views were mutually complementary, each with its theoretical value. Han Yu and Liu Zongyuan broke new ground with their literary theory and works, enriched the styles of classic Chinese literature with playful writing, and greatly influenced essay writing of later generations.

引例 Citations：

◎吾子又讥吾与人人为无实驳杂之说，此吾所以为戏耳。比之酒色，不有间

（jiàn）乎？吾子讥之，似同浴而讥裸裎（chéng）也。（韩愈《答张籍书》）
（您又讥笑我与人谈论一些驳杂且没有根据的说法，其实这正是我作的游戏笔墨罢了。这比之于沉湎酒色，不是有很大差别吗？您讥讽我，这就像同在一起洗浴，您却嘲笑我赤身裸体啊！）

Once again, you are laughing at me for engaging in random discussions not based on facts. But for me, that is just a playful writing. It is quite different from indulging in alcohol or the pleasures of the flesh. For you, to jeer at me is like laughing at my naked body when we are bathing together. (Han Yu: In Reply to Zhang Ji's Letter)

◎昌黎韩愈，仆识之旧矣……其人信美材也。近或闻诸侪类云：恃其绝足，往往奔放，不以文立制，而以文为戏。可矣乎？（裴度《寄李翱书》）
（昌黎韩愈，我认识他很久了……他确实很有才华。近来听一些朋友谈到他时都说：韩愈自负其不凡的才华，作文常常奔放不羁，他不以文章为社会创立规范，却将写文章看作游戏。这样做合适吗？）

I have known Han Yu for a long time... He is no doubt a talented man. These days, however, I have been told he has become complacent and often disregards all established rules in writing. He does not bother to set norms for society in his writing, treating it only as a way to amuse himself. Is that proper? (Pei Du: My Letter to Li Ao)

◎诗人视一切外物，皆游戏之材料也。然其游戏，则以热心为之。故诙谐与严重二性质，亦不可缺一也。（王国维《〈人间词话〉删稿》）
（诗人将一切外在事物都看作写作戏谑文字的素材。然而写这种戏谑文字，须有极大的热忱。因此，诙谐与庄重这两种特质，也是缺一不可的。）

A poet sees all external objects as materials for playful writing, but such writing requires keen interest. Therefore, wit and solemnity are both indispensable. (Wang Guowei: *Poetic Remarks in the Human World [The Deleted Part]*)

yìjìng-shénwàng 意静神王

A Tranquil Mind Is a Source of Inspiration.

意念清净，神思旺盛。“静”，指精神虚静，高度专一。王：通“旺”。是唐代诗僧皎然（720—796？）提出的诗学术语。它涉及诗歌的意境问题，描述的是灵感来临时，诗人意念高度清净专一，文思泉涌、有如神助的巅峰状态，与道家的“心斋”“坐忘”以及南朝刘勰（465？—520？或532？）所描述的“陶钧文思，贵在虚静”的创作状态是一脉相承的。

Here, *jing* (静) means being tranquil and focused, whereas *wang* (王) means "exuberant." Together, they describe a tranquil state of mind as being a source of inspiration. The term, first proposed by Jiaoran, a Tang Dynasty poet-monk (720-796?), sketches a highly creative state of mind that enables a poet to bring out his best. The term has much in common with the Daoist ideas of "pure state of the mind" or "forgetting the difference and opposition between self and the universe," as well as the tranquil and creative state of the mind described by Liu Xie (465?-520? or 532?) of the Southern Dynasties, which values "quiet emptiness of the mind" in conceiving a piece of writing.

引例 Citations:

◎有时意静神王，佳句纵横，若不可遏，宛若神助。（释皎然《诗式·取境》）

（有的时候意念清净，神思旺盛，佳句不断从胸中纵横而出，仿佛无法遏止，好似有神灵相助。）

When a poet is in a tranquil state of mind, he is able to give full rein to his imagination and write a stream of beautiful lines as if inspired by a divine being. (Shi Jiaoran: *Poetic Styles*)

◎是以陶钧文思，贵在虚静，疏瀹（yuè）五藏（zàng），澡雪精神。（刘勰《文心雕龙·神思》）

（因此构思文章，最重要的是虚静，不受外物干扰，身体舒泰如同五脏贯通了一样，精神洁净如同洗洁过一样。）

In conceiving an essay, one should strive for a mental state of quiet emptiness and not let oneself be bothered by external interferences, and be relaxed and at ease just like all his internal organs are put in perfect comfort and his spirits refreshed by a thorough wash. (Liu Xie: *The Literary Mind and the Carving of Dragons*)

yōngyīn-zátǐ 庸音杂体

Banal Content and Jumbled Forms

思想内容平庸、体制风格驳杂的文艺作品。“音”指表达心声的文字，特指诗句；“体”是根据内容确定的体裁、风格。钟嵘（？—518？）之所以提出这一批评术语，是针对当时有些青年诗人缺乏生活阅历和艺术经验，仅仅因为喜欢诗或羡慕诗人的风雅形象而写诗，其作品既缺乏真情实感和个人体悟，又没有明确的主旨与统一的情感基调，因此内容凌乱，风格驳杂。与钟嵘同时的刘勰（465？—520？或 532？）在《文心雕龙·宗经》中，也针对这种风气，提出了文学创作应当效法儒家经典的六条原则：“情深而不诡”（感情深厚而不欺诈），“风清而不杂”（风格清新而不杂乱），“事信而不诞”（记事真实而不虚妄），“义贞而不回”（道理正直而不邪曲），“体约而不芜”（体制简练而不芜杂），“文丽而不淫”（文辞华美而不浮靡）。

This term refers to works of art which are banal in content and jumbled in form. Here *yin* (音) stands for words from the heart in general and poetic creation in particular. *Ti* (体) refers to the choice of genre or style on the basis of content. Zhong Rong (?-518?) used this concept to criticize some young poets of his time who, lacking true feelings and personal experience, could only produce works ill-organized in content and form, devoid of any clear theme or core emotion. In his opinion, they wrote poetry only out of love or because they admired poets for their refinement. Zhong's contemporary Liu Xie (465?-520? or 532?) proposed six principles for emulating the creation of Confucian classics, in the chapter "Regarding Classics as Ultimate Sources" in his *The Literary Mind and the Carving of Dragons*. First, writing should be an outcome of deep feelings, not of guile. Second, it should be stylistically innovative without causing confusion. Third, it should truthfully record people and things rather than distort them. Fourth, it should abandon sophistry in favor of fair reasoning. Fifth, it should be neatly structured, not too wide-ranging. Sixth, it should be charming without any hint of decadence.

引例 Citations：

◎于是庸音杂体，人各为容，至使膏腴子弟，耻文不逮，终朝点缀，分夜呻吟。（钟嵘《诗品》卷上）

（此时有些诗人写的作品思想内容平庸、体制风格驳杂，却自以为作品很美，以至于一群贵胄子弟都以作品文采不及他人为耻，成天点缀文辞，大半夜还在吟诗。）

Works by some poets of today are banal in content and jumbled in form, but these poets still believe that their poems are truly beautiful. As a result, many children of noble birth regard lack of adornment in their poetic compositions as shameful. They are busy seeking out literary embellishment all day and go on chanting poems well into the night. (Zhong Rong: *The Critique of Poetry*)

◎故踸踔（chěnchuō）于短垣，放庸音以足曲。(陆机《文赋》)

([才分不足]就像仅有一条腿而要跳过矮墙一样，只好放任自己用平庸的文字去凑成篇章。)

Lack of talent is like a handicap trying to jump over a low wall with only one leg. All one can do is put some fine-sounding words together to produce a mediocre piece of writing. (Lu Ji: The Art of Writing)

yǒushàn 友善

Friendly and Kind

友好亲近，和善共处。"友"的古字形象方向相同的两只手，引申为志趣相同，互为援手；"善"本义美善、和善。两字联用，用来形容超越血缘的人与人之间亲密和善的关系状态。这种关系的建立是以彼此秉持共同的道义原则为前提的。时至今日，作为一种个人品质和伦理规范，它仍然被认为是构建和谐美好社会所必需的价值观。

This term means to be friendly and kind to each other in peaceful co-existence. *You* (友) in its ancient ideographic form consists of two hands extending in the same direction, metaphorically indicating common interest and offering a helping hand to each other. *Shan* (善) means to be gracious and kind. When these two Chinese characters are used together as in the current term, they denote a close and harmonious relationship among people, a bond that transcends blood ties. This kind of bond is based on the principle of righteousness commonly upheld by all parties involved. To date, as a hallmark of good character and ethical conduct, friendliness is still deemed as an essential element in the value system for building a harmonious and ideal society.

引例 Citations：

◎友者，所以相有也。道不同，何以相有也？……取友善人，不可不慎，是德之基也。（《荀子·大略》）

（朋友是用来互相帮助的。如果奉行的原则不同，靠什么来互相帮助呢？……选取朋友，共进于善，不可以不慎重，这是培养道德的基础。）

Friends are those who support each other if necessary. If they differ in principle, what can they depend on to help each other? ... Choosing friends should therefore be done with great care. That is the starting point for moral cultivation. (*Xunzi*)

◎君子先择而后交，小人先交而后择。（《文中子·魏相》）

（君子是先选择值得交往之人再去结交，一般人则是结交之后再选择［对自己是否有利］。）

A man of virtue selects a worthy individual first before making friends with him, whereas an ordinary man engages with people first before choosing those who would be beneficial to him. (*Wenzhongzi*)

yǒuxīnzhīqì 有心之器

Objects of Intelligence and Sentiment

本指有智慧情感的人，引申指由人类心灵智慧创制出来的文章及各种器物。无论是文章还是器物，它们都自然打上了人类精神创造的烙印，并带有外在的文采或纹饰。南朝刘勰（465？—520？ 或 532？ ）在《文心雕龙·原道》中指出，天地万物无不具有文德，即外在的形式美，“夫以无识之物，郁然有彩；有心之器，其无文欤？ ”从表面看这好像是疑问句，但实际上答案寓于问句之中，其肯定的态度是明显的。刘勰这一论断，指出了人类具有追求外在形式之美的天性，这是文学艺术作品以及文章形式之美得以产生的心理基础。

This term originally referred to intelligent and noble-minded human beings and later came to also cover the writings and articles created by them. These writings and articles were seen as embodying human vision, with literary grace or fine adornment. Liu Xie (465?-520? or 532?) of the Southern Dynasties, author of *The Literary Mind and the Carving of Dragons*, pointed out in the "Origin of Dao" section of that book the artistic grace, namely, the outward beauty, exists in all things in the world. "Since even non-human objects have a graceful style, how can humans, intelligent and full of vision, be without beautiful writing?" Liu's argument is made abundantly clear here, which is that humans are naturally inclined to pursue outward beauty. This is the psychological basis for the creation of beauty in literary and artistic works as well as literary styles.

引例 Citations:

◎夫以无识之物，郁然有彩；有心之器，其无文欤？（刘勰《文心雕龙·原道》）

（那些没有意识的东西，都有浓郁的文采；富有智慧情感的人类，怎能没有文章呢？）

Since even non-human objects have a graceful style, how can humans, intelligent and full of vision, go without beautiful writing? (Liu Xie: *The Literary Mind and the Carving of Dragons*)

◎［刚柔交错，］天文也。文明以止，人文也。（《周易·彖上》）

（［刚柔相互错杂，］是天的法则。礼仪昌明有所节制，是人伦的法则。）

It is a law of heaven that the hard and soft interweave; it is a rule of humans that they should observe the rites and conduct themselves with restraint. (*The Book of Changes*)

◎言之无文，行而不远。（《左传·襄公二十五年》）

（语言如果缺乏文采和技巧，就不可能流传广泛久远。）

Lackluster wording never travels far. (*Zuo's Commentary on The Spring and Autumn Annals*)

yúlùn 舆论

Public Opinion

众人的言论。“舆”的意思指众人、民众，“论”即议论、看法或意见。历来开明的执政者在决策形成之前都注重广泛采集众人包括普通民众的意见，并希望决策符合下情，以最大限度地保障决策的合理性和可行性。至近代，“舆论”与 public opinion 对译，成为有政治学、伦理学、社会心理学等多学科基础的概念，一般指代表社会大众或与国民意见一致的言论。古代“舆论”一词属于民本范畴，现代“舆论”一词属于民主范畴，两者本质相异，又可转换相通。

This term means widely held ideas and attitudes among the general public. The term is made up of two Chinese characters, with the first *yu* (舆) referring to the general public and the second *lun* (论) to commentaries, perspectives, or opinions. All wise rulers in history paid attention to consulting the general public for their opinions before making policy decisions, hoping that the resultant policy would meet the needs of the people and be rational and feasible. In modern times, the term is used as the Chinese equivalent of "public opinion" and generally refers to the views of people in the society or prevailing points of view reflective of what most people think. Therefore it has become a basic concept for many disciplines, such as politics, ethics, and social psychology. In ancient times, the term reflected the governing principle of "for the people." In modern times, however, it reflects the governing principle of "by the people." These two are different in nature, but are interchangeable and interrelated.

引例 Citations：

◎ 帝雅好儒士，留心贡举。有时微行人间，采听舆论，以观选士之得失。（《旧唐书·宣宗纪》）

（唐宣宗素来赏识儒士，留意科举的情况。他有时微服到民间访察，听取民众的议论，以便了解人才选拔是否得当。）

Emperor Xuanzong of Tang valued Confucian scholars very much and paid close attention to the selection of officials through imperial examinations. He would sometimes travel around in plain clothes to hear what people say so he could know whether the selections were well made. (*The Old Tang History*)

◎爰询廷臣，博采舆论，佥谓拯弊必合更张。（《元史·食货志五·钞法》）

（于是与朝中大臣商议，广泛听取众人的意见，他们都认为拯救弊端，必当改革。）

I have therefore discussed with the ministers to hear broadly their opinions. They all believe that reforms are necessary in order to redress the ills and wrongs. (*The History of the Yuan Dynasty*)

◎虽庙堂处分，未必尽协舆论；而缙绅公议，颇足维持世风。（《明史·马经纶传》）

（即便是朝廷的决定，也不一定都与大众的意见一致；而士大夫的共同看法，则足以维持社会风气。）

Even decisions by the imperial court may not be always in agreement with the public opinion. However, the general consensus by higher officials is enough to keep the social atmosphere healthy. (*The History of the Ming Dynasty*)

yuánshǒu 元首

Head of State

本义指人的头，比喻天子、君主。在古人看来，国家的权力结构好比人体，而君主则好比头脑，臣子好比肢体。君最尊贵，也很重要，甚至对国家的命运有决定性影响；但君臣又是一体的，他们相互依存，彼此配合，同理国事，荣辱与共。这种认识隐含国家有机整体论的萌芽。近代以降，该词仍指国家最高领导人，但其概念的外延扩大了，既包括世袭制的皇帝、国王等，也包括选举制的国家主席、总统等。

The term originally meant the head of a person. Metaphorically, it refers to the Son of Heaven, or the ruler. The ancient Chinese likened the power structure of a country to the body of a person, with the ruler functioning as its head, the officials as its body. The ruler was highly esteemed and the most important person, often exerting a crucial influence on the fate of a country. Yet, the ruler and his officials were parts of the same body. They depended on each other, worked collaboratively, handled state affairs together, and shared a common stake. Such an understanding was a nascent view that considered a country as an integral whole. Since modern times began, this term has come to mean the leader of a country, whether an emperor or a king who has inherited the throne, or the elected president of a country.

引例 Citations：

◎君为元首，臣为股肱，同体相须，共成美恶者也。（《后汉书·陈蕃传》）

（君王好比是人的脑袋，臣子好比是人的大腿和胳膊。他们是一个相互依存的整体，共同影响国家治理的好坏。）

The ruler is like the head of a person, and officials are like his arms and legs. They are mutually dependent parts of an organic whole, collectively responsible for the success or failure of a country's governance. (*The History of the Later Han Dynasty*)

◎夫（fú）帝王者，万国之元首，天下之所系命也。（《三国志·吴书·薛综传》）

（帝王是天下万国的元首，关系全天下人的命运。）

The emperor is the head of all the states under heaven, who determines the fate of all under heaven. (*The History of the Three Kingdoms*)

◎天子尊崇，故称元首；臣邻辅翼，故曰股肱。（程登吉《幼学琼林·朝廷》）

（天子地位尊贵，所以称“元首”；臣子居辅助地位，所以称“股肱”。）

The Son of Heaven reigns supreme, so he is called the head of state. His officials are likened the arms and legs because they assist him in exercising governance. (Cheng Dengji: *Scholarly Learning for Children*)

zǎocí-juéyù 藻辞谲喻

Richly Nuanced Wording and Intricate Figurative Meaning

辞藻华美而丰富，喻义委婉而多变。这是南朝刘勰（465？—520？或532？）在《文心雕龙·宗经》中对《诗经》创作特点的概括，亦代表了文学作品的审美特征：复杂深沉的情志难以用语言表达，需要运用丰富的辞藻和多种手法、技巧；有些意旨不能直言，需要运用婉转曲折的表达方式。因而文学作品既有令人目不暇接的丰富华美文辞，又有令人惊讶赞叹的巧妙手法，还有令人回味无穷的多重意蕴。

Wording should be refined and colorful whereas figurative meaning should be discreet and varied. Thus opined Liu Xie (465?-520? or 532?) of the Southern Dynasties, when he summarized the creative features of *The Book of Songs* in the chapter "Regarding Classics as Ultimate Sources" in *The Literary Mind and the Carving of Dragons*. It also represents the universal aesthetic feature of literary creation. Complex feelings and aspirations are difficult to express in a straightforward way, so a wider variety of wording and techniques of expression are needed. Some profound aspirations cannot be directly stated, and have to be expressed in a discreet way. Thus, literary works may embrace both beautiful and colorful wording, as well as surprising and ingenious techniques of expression. They may also contain a wealth of implicit messages.

引例 Citation：

◎《诗》主言志，诂训同《书》，摛（chī）《风》裁兴，藻辞谲喻，温柔在诵，故最附深衷矣。（刘勰《文心雕龙·宗经》）

（《诗经》主于抒发情志，其文字与《尚书》一样需要解释，《国风》等诗篇赋比兴等各种表现手法的运用，辞藻华美而丰富，喻义委婉而多变，吟诵时可以体会到它温柔敦厚的意蕴，所以它最能切合人的内心情感。）

The Book of Songs is to voice one's feelings and aspirations. As with *The Book of History*, its wording needs to be interpreted. "Ballads from the States" and other types of verses in *The Book of Songs* use different means of expression such as narrative, analogy, and association; their wording is beautiful and colorful; and their figurative meanings are discreet and richly nuanced. When these verses are chanted, one can feel a gentle kindness implicit in them. Therefore, they best suit the expression of people's inner feelings. (Liu Xie: *The Literary Mind and the Carving of Dragons*)

zhèng xiàng yuè, yuè cóng hé 政象乐，乐从和

Both Governance and Music Playing Pursue Harmony.

治理国家就像演奏音乐，而演奏音乐则要追求乐曲和谐。这一命题出自《国语·周语下》，是先秦乐论中的一个重要思想。它强调治理国家与演奏

音乐有共通之处。乐有五音，各种乐器不论声音大小高低，只有声音和谐平正，相互协调、彼此应和，方能成就完美的乐曲。治理国家亦是追求不同声音、不同力量的均平和谐。从音乐本身来说，“和”是不同声音的和谐与统一，并非声音完全相同。完全相同的声音，是单调无益的，而和谐的声音不仅提供愉悦的审美感受，还能有益于民众德行的培养，使其性情平和，最终有助于社会政治理想局面的形成。

Governance of a country is like playing music, which pursues harmony. This concept is first found in *Discourses on Governance of the States*. It is an important part of music theory from the pre-Qin period and highlights the similarity between the two. Traditional Chinese music contains five musical notes. Musical instruments, varying in volume, will not be deemed perfect unless they sound concordant and poised, complementing and echoing each other. In governing a country, the ruler should also strike an equilibrium between different voices and forces. So far as music itself is concerned, "harmony" does not mean homogeneity; rather, it refers to a diversity of melodies integrated into a harmonious whole. A uniform voice is unpleasant and dull. A harmonious voice, on the other hand, not only provides a delightful aesthetic experience but also enhances people's moral well-being. This will make them mild in temperament, thus creating an ideal situation of social and political stability.

引例 Citations：

◎夫政象乐，乐从和，和从平。声以和乐，律以平声。（《国语·周语下》）

（治理国家就像演奏音乐，演奏音乐则要追求乐曲和谐，而乐曲和谐则要音声均平。声音的高低使乐曲和谐，乐调的不同则使声音均平。）

To achieve harmony, a musician maintains an equilibrium between different parts of a composition. Variation in levels of sound makes the melody harmonious, and alternation in pitch creates an overall effect of proportionality. A ruler governs his country in much the same way. (*Discourses on Governance of the States*)

◎和平则久，久固则纯，纯明则终，终复则乐，所以成政也，故先王贵之。（《国语・周语下》）

（声音和谐均平才能演奏持久，演奏持久稳定才能声音纯正，声音纯正明晰才能奏完一遍，然后从头开始循环往复才成就完整的乐曲，明白这个道理就可以成就政事，所以先王十分重视音律的和谐 。）

Maintaining a balance between voices allows a musical performance to run its own natural course. This, in turn, makes that performance sound pure. Purity and clarity help the progress of the music until the whole piece is completed. A ruler who understands this will run his country well. Therefore the ancient kings placed great value on musical harmony. (*Discourses on Governance of the States*)

zhīnán-xíngyì 知难行易

To Act Is Easy; To Know Is Hard.

对人伦日用之道的践行并不困难，真正的困难在于认知其道。这是对“知”“行”关系的又一种认识，与“知易行难”的观念相对。这一观念由孙中山（1866—1925）在《孙文学说》（后作为《建国方略》一书中的“心理建设”部分）中提出。在孙中山看来，传统的“知易行难”观念在当时已经成为禁锢人们思想、阻碍革命行动的“心理之大敌”。为了反对和破除这种传统的知行观念，他提出“知易行难”，强调求得真知以指导行动的重要意义。

This term suggests that it is not difficult to act according to general moral principles; what is truly difficult is to appreciate them. This is a different understanding of the relationship between knowledge and action, which stands in contrast with the view that "to know is easy; to act is hard." This idea was put forward by Sun Yat-sen (1866-1925) in his *Sun Wen's Theory* which was later incorporated into his *The Fundamentals of National Reconstruction* as the "Psychological Preparation" section. As Sun Yat-sen saw it, the traditional concept that "to know is easy; to act is hard" had by that time become a psychological barrier which both fettered people's thinking and hindered revolutionary action. He thus proposed the view that "to act is easy; to know is hard" in opposition to the traditional view of knowledge and action, and emphasized the importance of gaining true knowledge to guide one's action.

引例 Citations：

◎夫中国近代之积弱不振、奄奄待毙者，实为“知之非艰，行之惟艰”一说误之也。(《孙文学说》第五章“知行总论”)

（中国近代之所以长期孱弱而到了生命垂危的阶段，实质上就是“认识并不困难，付诸行动才难”这一错误说法造成的。）

The reason why China in the modern times has become so weak, to the point where its very existence is in peril is because it has been misled by the view that "it is not hard to know; what is truly hard is to act." (*Sun Wen's Theory*)

◎故天下事惟患于不能知耳，倘能由科学之理则以求得其真知，则行之决无所难。(《孙文学说》第五章“知行总论”)

（所以，最需要忧虑的是不能了解天下的事物，如果能够遵循科学的规律，求得天下事物的正确认识，那么付诸行动一定不会有什么困难。）

Thus what is of the greatest concern to us is not understanding the world. If we can follow the principles of science and acquire a true understanding of the world, then it will definitely not be difficult for us to act on this understanding. (*Sun Wen's Theory*)

zhītiān 知天

Understanding Heaven

知晓天对人的意义。在中国古人的思想中，“天”具有不同含义，以不同的方式对人事发挥着不可抗拒的影响。因此，“知天”就成为人们在天的影响下，把握自我与生活世界的关键。由于“天”的含义及天人关系的复杂性，“知天”也有着不同的方式和途径。如孟子（前372？—前289）认为，应通过充分实现天赋的善端来“知天”；荀子（前313？—前238）则认为，在礼的规范之下恰当地满足天生的身体官能的需求即是“知天”。

The term means to know heaven's significance to people. To the ancient Chinese thinkers, "heaven" could mean different things, and it has an inexorable impact on human affairs in various ways. Hence, given heaven's influence, it is crucial for people to understand heaven if they are to control themselves and the world in which they live. Because of the complexities in the meaning of heaven and in the relationship between heaven and humans, there are also different forms and paths for understanding heaven. For example, Mencius (372?-289 BC) felt that one could understand heaven by fully realizing the innate goodness in one's nature, whereas Xunzi (313?-238 BC) felt that understanding heaven meant appropriately meeting the needs of one's natural physical functions in a way which accorded with the rules of propriety.

引例 Citations：

◎孟子曰："尽其心者，知其性也。知其性，则知天矣。存其心，养其性，所以事天也。夭寿不贰，修身以俟之，所以立命也。"（《孟子·尽心上》）

（孟子言："能做到尽心的人，能知晓其本性。能知晓人的本性，则能够知晓天。保持自己的本心，培养自己的本性，就是对待天命的方法。无论短命长寿都不改变，修养身心以等待上天的安排，这就是确立天命的态度。"）

Mencius said, "He who does his utmost knows his nature. Knowing his nature, he understands heaven. Preserving his mind and nurturing his nature is the way to deal with the mandate of heaven. This does not change regardless of whether his life is long or short. He cultivates himself and awaits heaven's arrangements – this is the way to abide by the mandate of heaven." (*Mencius*)

◎其行曲治，其养曲适，其生不伤，夫是之谓知天。（《荀子·天论》）

（人们的行事都治理得当，对身体官能的供养也很适当，人的生命不受伤害，这就可以称得上"知天"。）

When one's affairs are properly handled, when one's body is properly nourished, when one's life is not harmed – then he can be said to understand heaven. (*Xunzi*)

zhīyán 知言

Discerning Statements

察知言辞的真意。早期儒家的《论语》《孟子》等文献中都提到"知言"的观念。儒家认为，言辞是人们表达和交流的中介。但由于种种原因，很多时候言辞并不能准确、真实、完整地传达意义。因此儒家强调要善于辨察言辞偏离真意的原因，并在此基础之上进一步探究言辞的真意。

This term means to discern the true meaning of statements. This concept is mentioned in early Confucian classics such as *The Analects* and *Mencius*. Confucianism regarded statements as the vehicle through which people express themselves and communicate with others. However, for various reasons, statements often cannot accurately, faithfully or fully convey the true meaning that was intended to convey. Hence Confucianism emphasized the need to discern statements to find out why they deviated from the true meaning and further explore it.

引例 Citations：

◎不知言，无以知人也。(《论语·尧曰》)

（不善于分辨别人的话，就不能真正地了解他。）

If you do not discern statements of others, you cannot understand them. (*The Analects*)

◎“何谓知言？”曰：“诐（bì）辞知其所蔽，淫辞知其所陷，邪辞知其所离，遁辞知其所穷。”(《孟子·公孙丑上》)

（公孙丑问：“什么是知言？”孟子说：“偏颇的言辞知道它片面的地方，浮夸的言辞知道它失实的地方，邪异的言辞知道它偏离正道的地方，搪塞的言辞知道它理屈词穷的地方。”）

Gongsun Chou asked, “What does discerning statements mean?” Mencius said, “Discerning statements enables one to know how one-sided statements are biased, exaggerations are untrue, heresy is deviated from truth and poor defense is unjustified.” (*Mencius*)

zhīyì-xíngnán 知易行难

To Know Is Easy; To Act Is Hard.

对人伦日用之道的认知并不困难，真正的困难在于践行其道。这是中国古人对“知”“行”关系的一种认识，与“知难行易”的观念相对。《左传》及古文《尚书》都提到过这种观念。这种知行观念将人的认知与行动视为既相区别又相联系的两个环节，并通过对“行”的困难的强调，避免知行脱节、知而不行的情况。

It is not difficult to know the moral principles guiding daily life; what is difficult is to practice them. This was a way with which the ancient Chinese dealt with the relationship between knowledge and action. This approach stood in contrast with the belief that action is easy whereas knowing is hard. This concept is mentioned in both *Zuo's Commentary on The Spring and Autumn Annals* and the “old text” version of *The Book of History*. Such a view of knowledge and action regards human knowledge and actions as both separate and interlinked. By emphasizing the difficulty of acting, it seeks to avoid a disconnect between knowledge and action.

引例 Citations：

◎非知之实难，将在行之。(《左传·昭公十年》)

（并不是难在“知”，而是难在“行”。）

To know is not the hard part; to act is. (*Zuo's Commentary on The Spring and Autumn Annals*)

◎非知之艰，行之惟艰。(《尚书·说（yuè）命中》)

（认识并不困难，付诸行动才难。）

Knowing is not hard; what is hard is acting. (*The Book of History*)

zhízhì 直致

Direct Expression

诗歌的描写或语言直接而不婉曲。致：到，抵达。与南朝钟嵘（？—518？）提出的“直寻”含义接近。钟嵘不满于有的诗歌搬用典故，认为诗歌是感于外物、吟咏情性之作，写景抒情应有真切的审美感受，语言表达应当不假雕饰、生动鲜明。唐代诗论家殷璠（fán）继承了钟嵘的观点，提出了“直致”，进一步说明诗歌写景抒情应当直接使用质朴率真、明朗自然的语言，传达自己的眼中之美、心中之情。

This term means that the description and language used in poetry should be direct and straight forward rather than implied. Here, *zhi* (致) means reaching to something. The origin of this term may be traced to the concept of direct search first proposed by Zhong Rong (?-518?) of the Southern Dynasties. He disapproved of the excessive use of allegories in some poems, maintaining that a poem could only be written when a poet was inspired by external objects. Whether describing scenery or expressing his thoughts, the poet should present his sentiments with vivid writing while avoiding the use of rhetoric. Yin Fan, a Tang Dynasty critic of poetry who followed Zhong Rong's view, put forward the term "direct expression," believing that one should use simple, clear and vivid language to describe both scenery and his sentiment.

引例 Citations:

◎观古今胜语，多非补假，皆由直寻。（钟嵘《诗品》卷中）

（综观古今名篇佳句，大都不是借用前人诗句或使用典故，而是直接从自身体验中寻求而得。）

An examination of well-known poetic works of both the past and the present shows that most of such poems hardly quote lines of classic poetry or literary allusions. Rather, they are directly inspired by the personal experiences of poets. (Zhong Rong: *The Critique of Poetry*)

◎至如曹刘，诗多直致，语少切对。（殷璠《河岳英灵集序》）

（至于说到曹操、刘桢，他们的诗作直接而不婉曲，很少注意形式上的平仄工整。）

The poems of Cao Cao and Liu Zhen are direct rather than implied in style, and these two poets cared little about tonal harmony. (Yin Fan: Preface to *A Collection of Poems by Distinguished Poets*)

zhǐshì-zàoxíng, qióngqíng-xiěwù 指事造形，穷情写物

Establish Relations Among Things, Create Images, Fully Explore Feelings and Aptly Depict External Things

指明事理，创造形象，穷尽情性，描摹事物。指诗歌的写作手法。“指事造形”是形象地描写，对于景物、人物等，能传达外在的形貌特征，做到形似，令人、物如在目前；对于事理，能清楚准确地给予描述。“指事造形”与“穷情写物”密不可分。“穷情”，一方面指诗人写作需倾注激情、热情、

深情，托物寄情，唯有用情，方能写出感人的作品；另一方面，“穷情”也指努力穷尽事物之情，探究、揣摩人物、事物、景物的情态物理，如此方可写出神韵，而不致流于表面形似。“指事造形”与“穷情写物”相结合，就能使诗歌具体可感、生动传神。

These are the techniques used in writing poetry. The establishment of relations among things means that when depicting scenery and human figures, the poet should convey their outward features faithfully, making them look as if emerging right before readers' eyes. Besides, the poet should demonstrate the implications of things clearly and accurately. The establishment of relations among things and the creation of imagery are inseparable from full exploration of the nuances of feelings and apt depiction of scenery and things. On the one hand, the poet should write with all his passion and devotion, embodying his feelings in external objects. Only true feelings can produce profoundly moving poetry. On the other hand, the poet should pursue underlying implications to the utmost, exploring the spiritual as well as the physical state of human figures, objects and scenery. In doing so, he is able to infuse a poetic charm and vigor into his work, free from a superficial resemblance to the things depicted. Linking the creation of relations and imagery with a description of objects and feelings makes poetry more tangible and vivid.

引例 Citations：

◎五言居文词之要，是众作之有滋味者也。故云会于流俗，岂不以指事造形，穷情写物，最为详切者邪？（钟嵘《诗品》卷上）

（五言诗在各种诗体中居于首位，是众多作品中最有审美意味的。所以说它合乎流行的审美风气，难道不是因为它是指明事理、创造形象、穷尽情感、描摹事物最为详尽恰切的一种文体吗？）

Five-character-per-line poems constitute the most important poetic form and are most richly imbued with nuanced flavors. We say that they comply with the prevalent aesthetic taste of today simply because they establish relations among things, create images, fully explore feelings and aptly depict external things, don't they? (Zhong Rong: *The Critique of Poetry*)

◎凡作诗，须知道紧要下手处，便了当得快也。其法有三：曰事，曰情，曰景。（谢榛《四溟诗话》卷四）

（凡是作诗，必须知道在最关键的地方下手，就能干脆快速写成了。其方法有三个：事理、情感、景物。）

As long as one knows the key elements, one will be able to produce a poem quickly. There are three things to do: establish relations among things, explore human feelings, and portray scenery and objects. (Xie Zhen: *Siming's Remarks on Poetry*)

zhìlǐ-zuòyuè 制礼作乐

Establish Rites and Compose Music

制定礼法，创作音乐。“礼”“乐”是用以规范个人与他人、与天地万物乃至与鬼神之间关系的一整套社会秩序，包含着有关器物、仪式、制度等不同层面的设计与规定。儒家认为，其所继承的周代礼乐，是先王依据对天道、人情的把握而创作、制定的，体现着先王对天道与人情的遵从和安顿。

Li (rites) and *yue* (music) are a whole set of social norms for regulating individuals' conduct and their relationships with other people as well as everything else in nature and even ghosts and spirits. These norms involve ceremonial vessels, rituals, and systems which were designed and established for various levels. Confucianism believes that the social norms featuring rituals and music of the Zhou Dynasty were established and created by the kings of the time according to their understanding of natural laws and human sentiment. Such social norms epitomize their respect and proper expressions of the law of nature and human feelings.

引例 Citation:

◎武王崩，成王幼弱，周公践天子之位，以治天下。六年，朝诸侯于明堂，制礼作乐，颁度量，而天下大服。(《礼记·明堂位》)

（周武王去世，周成王年幼弱小，周公履行天子的职位，以治理天下。第六年，召诸侯在明堂朝见天子，并制定礼乐，颁布度量的标准，因而天下十分信服。）

King Wu of the Zhou Dynasty died and his successor King Cheng was still very young, so the Duke of Zhou performed the duties of governing the country on King Cheng's behalf. In the sixth year, the Duke of Zhou summoned all heads of dukedoms to the Hall of Brightness to establish social norms in the form of rituals and music and promulgate standard measurements. He thus commanded the allegiance of the entire country. (*The Book of Rites*)

zhìbìng-jiùrén 治病救人

Treat the Illness and Save the Patient

治疗疾病，挽救生命。使人摆脱危险和痛苦、恢复健康，这是医疗的本质属性，也是医者崇尚的宗旨或理念，体现了医者尊重人的生命的悲悯情怀和人文精神。现在也多用来比喻针对人的缺点或错误进行批评或处分，促使其克服缺点，改正错误。批评或处分只是手段，而且对事不对人，目的是要把有缺点或错误的人拉回正确的轨道上来。这体现了在对待他人缺点、错误方面，坚持原则与宽以待人精神的有机统一，与“爱人以德”不无渊源。

Ridding people of danger and suffering and enabling them to recover their health is the essential nature of medical treatment. It is also the noble aspiration or ideal of the physician, and it exemplifies the physician's compassionate respect for human life and the humanistic spirit. This expression is now also used as an analogy in pointing out someone's shortcomings or mistakes when criticizing or penalizing them, to enable them to overcome their shortcomings and correct their mistakes. Criticisms or penalties are merely measures taken to help someone; they target the behavior and not the person, and the goal is to bring someone with shortcomings or mistakes back onto the right path. This demonstrates the organic unity of firmly adhering to principles while showing leniency towards the person, and it is related to the concept "loving the people in accordance with rules of moral conduct."

引例 Citation:

◎沈羲，吴郡人，学道于蜀，能治病救人，甚有恩德。（《太平御览・道部四・天仙》）

（沈羲，吴郡人，在蜀地学得道术，能治病救人，医德和口碑都非常好。）

Shen Xi was a native of Wu Prefecture. Having learned Daoist practices in Sichuan, he could treat illnesses and save people, and had excellent medical ethics and reputation. (*Imperial Reader for Emperor Taizong of the Song Dynasty*)

zìshèng 自胜

Overcome Oneself

战胜自我，克制自己。人有长短，事有成败。而事之成，取决于己之长；事之败，取决于己之短。通过自身的不断努力，不断地消除自身的不足，超越自身的局限，使自己无限地趋于完善，成为真正的强者。这不仅是克服困难、战胜敌人的先决条件，也是个人提升自我的生命历程。一人如此，一国亦如此。其基本精神与“自强不息”不无相通之处。

Overcoming oneself means to conquer and control oneself. Everybody has his strengths and weaknesses, and he may succeed or fail in what he does. One's strengths and skills bring success, whereas one's weaknesses lead to failure. Therefore, one needs to make constant efforts to improve oneself, overcome one's weaknesses, transcend one's limitations, and eventually become a truly capable person. This is not only a prerequisite for overcoming particular difficulties and defeating enemies, but also a lifetime pursuit for a better self. This is true for a person and for a country as well. The aspiration embodied therein is similar to what is expressed in the term "strive continuously to strengthen oneself."

引例 Citations:

◎胜人者有力，自胜者强。(《老子・三十三章》)

（战胜别人的是有力量，战胜自我的才是真正的强大。）

Those who conquer others are strong, but those who conquer themselves are truly powerful. (*Laozi*)

◎能胜强敌者，先自胜者也。（《商君书·画策》）

（能战胜强大对手的人，是那些首先战胜自己的人。）

Those who can conquer powerful enemies are those who conquer themselves first. (*The Book of Lord Shang*)

◎故欲胜人者，必先自胜。（《吕氏春秋·先己》）

（所以要想战胜别人，必须首先战胜自己。）

Therefore, one must conquer oneself before conquering others. (*Master Lü's Spring and Autumn Annals*)

zìxìn 自信

Believe in One's Self

相信自己。即对自己的想法、做法等的正确性、正当性由衷地抱持坚定信心，在任何情况下，都会坚定不移地为之努力，绝不放弃自己的信念和目标，不含糊动摇，不屈己就人。自信的前提是自我诚信，只有做到了自我诚信，才能给予自己强大的信心，也才能得到他人的信任。“自信”所强调的是主体性的树立，与“自强不息”精神相通。

Have trust in one's self so that one strongly believes in the correctness and validity of one's thoughts and actions. One who has such a belief will give up neither one's conviction nor one's goals. He will neither waver nor submit to others. A strong sense of personal integrity underlies this sense of self-belief, which in turn wins the trust of others. The term expresses a sense of self, and relates closely to the concept "strive continuously to strengthen oneself."

引例 Citations：

◎自疑不信人，自信不疑人。（《素书·安礼》）

（自己怀疑自己，就不会信任别人；自己相信自己，就不会怀疑别人。）

Doubt in one's self leads to doubt of others; belief in one's self leads to belief in others. (Huangshigong's Strategies on White Silk)

◎自信者不可以诽誉迁也，知足者不可以势利诱也。（《淮南子·诠言训》）

（对于自信的人，是不能用诽谤或赞誉来改变他的；对于知足的人，是不能用权势和利益来诱惑他的。）

One who has self-belief cannot be changed by either slander or praise; one who is satisfied cannot be tempted by either power or profit. (*Huainanzi*)

◎天道最公，人能苦心，断不负苦心，为善者须当自信。（王永彬《围炉夜话》）

（上天的法则最是公平，人能尽心尽力，一定不会被上天辜负，行善的人应当自信。）

The rules of heaven are fair, and those who try their hardest will not be disappointed. Those who do good should believe in themselves. (Wang Yongbin: *Night Talks Around the Hearth*)

zìzhī 自知

Know One's Self / Self-knowledge

认识自己，了解自己的长处和短处。这是正确认识他人及一切事物的基础，也是不断超越自我、提升自我的前提。它往往是有智慧的人与杰出者的基本素质。它强调的是人的自我意识的觉醒、主体精神的树立，与古希腊“认识你自己”的理念相通。

The term means to have knowledge and understanding of one's strengths and weaknesses. This is the basis for knowing others and all other things. Further self-improvement and progress stem from this. Exceptional and wise people often demonstrate this quality. The focus is on developing a conscious sense of self, which echoes the ancient Greek axiom "know thyself."

引例 Citations：

◎知人者智，自知者明。(《老子·三十三章》)

（善于了解别人，算得上有智慧；善于了解自己，才算得上圣明。）

Knowing others is wisdom; knowing one's self is insight. (*Laozi*)

◎自知者不怨人，知命者不怨天。怨人者穷，怨天者无志。失之己，反之人，岂不迂乎哉！（《荀子·荣辱》）

（有自知之明的人不会埋怨别人，懂得天命的人不会埋怨老天。只会埋怨别人的人会招致窘困，只会埋怨老天的人会失去志向。错在自己，却责怪别人，难道不觉得荒唐吗？）

Those who have knowledge of their selves do not blame others; those who understand the will of heaven do not blame it. Blaming others creates difficulties for one's self; blaming heaven saps one's aspirations. Is it not ridiculous to blame others for one's own mistakes? (*Xunzi*)

◎故欲胜人者，必先自胜；欲论人者，必先自论；欲知人者，必先自知。(《吕氏春秋·先己》)

（所以，如果想要战胜他人，必须先要战胜自己；如果想要评论他人，必须先要评论自己；如果想要了解他人，必须先要了解自己。）

Therefore, to conquer others first conquer yourself, to comment on others first comment on yourself, and to know others first know yourself. (*Master Lü's Spring and Autumn Annals*)

zìzhì 自治

Self-discipline / Self-control

自己治理自己，包括修养自身德行、约束自己行为、管理自己事务等含义。在政治上，它属于"人治"范畴。它要求治理者顺应形势严格管好自己，以身作则，然后带动广大民众管好自己及自己的事情，进而达成整个社会的良好治理状态。近代以来，人们用它与 autonomy 和 self-government 对译，使"自治"一词演变为政治概念，指依据法律规定，在一个国家内，民族、地区、团体等除了受所隶属的国家、政府或上级单位领导外，行政上相对独立，对自己的事务可以独立行使一定的权力，如"地方自治""民族区域自治"等。

The ability to control one's self includes cultivating one's mind, controlling one's behavior, and managing one's affairs. Politically, it falls into the category of "rule by man," in which the ruler exercises strict self-discipline and sets an example, so that the people also manage their affairs properly. This leads to positive social governance. In modern times, *zizhi* (自治) is used as the counterpart of "autonomy" or "self-government," so it has become a political concept. It means that, within a state, ethnic groups, geographic regions and civil groupings have a certain amount of administrative independence while still following national, government and organizational regulations, e.g., "local autonomy," and "regional ethnic autonomy."

引例 Citations：

◎是故明君知民之必以上为心也，故置法以自治，立仪以自正也。(《管子・法法》)

（因此，贤明的君王知道百姓一定是以君王的喜好为中心的，所以制定法度用来治理自己，树立礼仪用来规正自己。）

Therefore, a wise ruler knows that since the people will follow his preferences, norms and rules to guide and limit his personal thought and action must be set. (*Guanzi*)

◎故百姓则君以自治也。(《礼记・礼运》)

（所以，百姓都是效法国君来达到自我治理的。）

Therefore, the people will emulate the ways of the ruler to manage themselves. (*The Book of Rites*)

◎夫治民与自治，治彼与治此，治小与治大，治国与治家，未有逆而能治之也，夫惟顺而已矣。(《黄帝内经・灵枢・师传》)

（治理百姓和治理自身，统治这里和统治那里，处理小事和处理大事，治理国家与治理家庭，从没有违背事理而能治理好的，只有顺应事理才能治理好。）

Whether managing others or controlling one's self, ruling here or there, dealing with small or large matters, governing the country or directing a household, success depends on conforming to concrete conditions, otherwise all efforts will fail. (*Yellow Emperor's Internal Canon of Medicine*)